Constructing and Covering Boxes:
A Beginner's Guide

Tom and Cindy Hollander

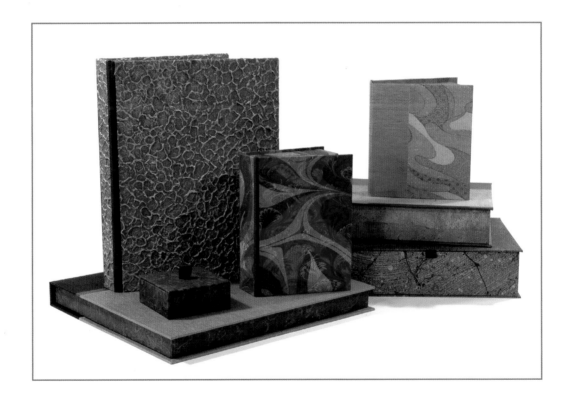

Schiffer Publishing Ltd ®

4880 Lower Valley Road, Atglen, Pa 19310

Dedication

This book is dedicated to Annette Hollander, Tom's mother. From the late 1960s through the 1970s, Annette successfully developed a unique craft business she called *Bookcraft*. She used many of the basic materials, tools, and techniques of traditional bookbinding to make and cover boxes and various desk accessories with decorative papers. An accomplished artist, Annette also taught herself how to make unique decorative papers, which she often used in her work.

Annette wrote two books during the early 1970s. The first was *Decorative Papers and Fabrics*, published in 1971 by the Van Nostrand Reinhold Company. Her second book, *Bookcraft*, was published in 1974 by the Van Nostrand Reinhold Company and later reprinted by Dover Publishing under the title *Easy to Make Desk Accessories*.

Annette was ahead of her time, and we consider her one of the earliest pioneers of the current book and paper arts movement. At 88 years old, she is still active and creative. When we told her we were writing this book and asked her to make a few "special" boxes for it, she was thrilled.

Several of Annette's boxes, such as the Butterfly Box pictured below, are featured in the **Creative Boxes** chapter.

Without Annette's creative inspiration, enthusiasm, support, and encouragement over the past forty years, this book would not have been possible.

Butterfly Box with Double Hinged Lid, 9 1/2" x 14 1/2" x 1 1/2". Made by Annette Hollander

Other Schiffer Books on Related Subjects
Turning Boxes with Friction-Fitted Lids. Bill Bowers.
ISBN: 9780764330278. $14.99

Designed by RoS
Type set in Futura Hv BT/Dutch 809 BT

ISBN: 978-0-7643-3158-9
Printed in China

Schiffer Books are available at special discounts for bulk purchases for sales promotions or premiums. Special editions, including personalized covers, corporate imprints, and excerpts can be created in large quantities for special needs. For more information contact the publisher:

Published by Schiffer Publishing Ltd.
4880 Lower Valley Road
Atglen, PA 19310
Phone: (610) 593-1777; Fax: (610) 593-2002
E-mail: Info@schifferbooks.com

For the largest selection of fine reference books on this and related subjects, please visit our web site at **www.schifferbooks.com**
We are always looking for people to write books on new and related subjects. If you have an idea for a book please contact us at the above address.

This book may be purchased from the publisher.
Include $5.00 for shipping.
Please try your bookstore first.
You may write for a free catalog.

In Europe, Schiffer books are distributed by
Bushwood Books
6 Marksbury Ave.
Kew Gardens
Surrey TW9 4JF England
Phone: 44 (0) 20 8392-8585; Fax: 44 (0) 20 8392-9876
E-mail: info@bushwoodbooks.co.uk
Website: www.bushwoodbooks.co.uk
Free postage in the U.K., Europe; air mail at cost.

All boxes in this book were made by Tom and Cindy Hollander unless otherwise noted.
Digital photographs by Tom Hollander.

Acknowledgments

This book would not have been possible without the long-term support of Annette Hollander, Tom's mother; for all of her encouragement, we are greatly appreciative. We would like to express our gratitude to Maureen Hollander, Tom's sister, for her expertise and advice in reviewing the manuscript. In addition, we would like to thank Monique Lallier, Don Etherington, Jeff Snyder, Cheryl MacKrell, and Jessica Hollander, Tom and Cindy's daughter, for taking the time to review the book and offer many constructive comments.

We would especially like to acknowledge the long time support of our many customers, students, and staff. Without them, we would not be where we are today and in a position to write this book. Finally, we would like to thank the Kerrytown Shops in Ann Arbor for supporting our vision and providing us with such a unique setting in which to grow for the past seventeen years.

Hinged Lid Box, open.

Hinged Lid Box, closed, 8" x 10" x 2 1/4".

Contents

Foreword

Boxes are fascinating! Everyone loves them and as you will soon discover, they can be made in many different sizes, shapes, and with various materials. Boxes are especially meaningful when you can make them yourself and also when you can give them to others as a gift. Once the basics of box making are learned, you will begin to conceptualize your own boxes and working with materials you never knew existed. After making several boxes and understanding the basics, you will feel much more comfortable and begin making your own, more creative boxes.

We are honored to write this foreword for Tom and Cindy Hollander's book because it is a very good guide to box making and has clear instructions and colorful pictures. We know that it also fills an important gap for beginners. By using this book, box making will be an inspiration to both young and old. Enjoy making your beautiful boxes!

— Monique Lallier and Don Etherington

Monique Lallier is internationally recognized as a major award-winning fine design bookbinder and book artist. For twelve years she was the Chairman of the Standards of Excellence of the Guild of Book Workers. She is the current director of the American Academy of Bookbinding.

Don Etherington is one of the most widely recognized names in fine binding and conservation. He is the founder of the Etherington Conservation Center in North Carolina and co-author of the book, *Boxes for the Protection of Rare Books: Their Design and Construction.*

Preface

Constructing and Covering Boxes: A Beginner's Guide is the result of two related events. First, we recognized that there are virtually no books available that are devoted solely to the craft of box making. Occasionally a book on bookbinding devotes a few pages to making a box, such as a slipcase to hold a book. However, extensive step-by-step instructions for making high quality boxes are scant. We felt a book devoted to the basics of constructing and covering traditional style boxes was long overdue.

The second event was meeting Peter Schiffer, Jr. of Schiffer Publishing Ltd. While visiting our retail store in Ann Arbor, Michigan, Peter saw several of our box making booklets, based on the workshops we have been teaching and have been self-publishing for a number of years. Peter was enthusiastic about having us turn these booklets into a more definitive, how-to book, and encouraged us to write an instructional box making book geared towards the beginner. He suggested that the focus be less on a wide variety of box styles and more on a thorough, step-by-step approach for making one or two basic structures.

Having made well over a thousand boxes in the past twenty-five years, we felt the challenge to formalize a basic and thorough instruction book for beginners would be a rewarding undertaking and an important contribution to the craft field in general.

Hinged Lid Boxes, 5 1/2" x 7 1/2" x 2" and 8" x 10" x 2 1/4".

Clamshell Boxes, 6 3/4" x 8 1/2" x 1 1/2", 6" x 13" x 1 1/2", and 5" x 13" x 3/4".

Introduction

Constructing and Covering Boxes: A Beginners Guide is a step-by-step approach to learning the basic techniques for making high quality decorative and functional boxes. All of our boxes are constructed using book board, which is then covered with a combination of decorative papers and book cloth. Once the basics of box making are learned, a number of options and variations are available to explore and create more elaborate boxes.

This book describes techniques in box making that we have been practicing and teaching for over twenty-five years. Whenever we could simplify or improve the process of making boxes, we did so and incorporated them into our instructions. None of our methods are set in stone and after a while, intuition will enable you to come up with your own short cuts and techniques.

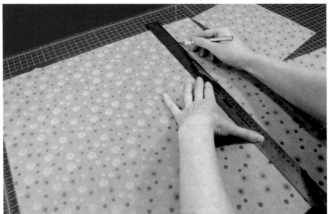

Terminology is helpful in describing any craft. We have tried to make our descriptions as easy to read as possible and to illustrate our descriptions with many pictures. Certain terms such as *turn-in* and *mitered corner* are useful for describing various steps, and we introduce these where appropriate.

Chapter 1 Materials and Tools, covers the basic materials, supplies, and tools that are commonly used in box making. Most of the tools are inexpensive and easy to acquire. Some materials may be a little more difficult to find, such as book board and book cloth. We list a number of reliable sources in the back of the book to help you find some of these.

Chapter 2 Basic Methods, discusses grain direction of materials, how to lay out your patterns, cutting, and gluing techniques and considerations.

Chapter 3 Hinged Lid Box, illustrates the step-by-step process for making the first of two basic box styles presented in this book. The lid is made separate from the tray, which is then attached to the bottom of the lid and the spine. The cover opens and closes along a hinge, much like a cigar box. This style of box can be made in a variety of sizes and is ideal for use on any desktop, coffee table, bookshelf, or nightstand. We have designed hinged lid boxes to hold pencils and pens, magazines, photos, CDs, playing cards, jewelry, chess pieces, remote controls, and almost anything imaginable.

From Top:
Divided Hinged
Lid Box with Three
Compartments, 3" x 13"
x 1 1/4".

Measuring and cutting
decorative paper.

Hinged Lid Box, closed,
5 1/2" x 7 1/2" x 2".

Hinged Lid Box, open.

Chapter 4 Clamshell Box, is the step-by-step process for making the second style of box we present in this book. Commonly called a clamshell box, it is also referred to as a two-tray drop spine box and sometimes a portfolio box. This box consists of a pair of three-sided trays, with one constructed slightly larger than the other. Each tray is attached to the lid with the open side facing inward or towards the spine. When the box is open, the spine drops, allowing the box to lay flat. When closed, the small tray nests inside the large tray, creating a double wall and a solid, protective structure. This style of box is most often used to hold a book or a loose collection of papers, photographs, or artwork. As with the hinged lid box, the clamshell box can be made to any dimension.

Clamshell Box, closed, 6 3/4" x 8 1/2" x 1 1/2".

Clamshell Box, open, with Journal.

Chapter 5 Creative Boxes, illustrates a number of box variations, added elements, and creative possibilities. Although detailed instructions are not a part of this chapter, most of the additions or variations we have shown can be figured out with some trial and error. The purpose of this chapter is to offer inspiration through a gallery of images.

Chapter 6 Box Making Formulas, is devoted to the formulas we use for making the hinged lid and clamshell styles. This chapter is useful for creating your own custom size boxes and includes sample worksheets that can be photo copied. These formulas may be modified based on your own measuring preferences. For example, we may round up or down by 1/16" so that we can cut in 1/8" increments.

A **Glossary of Terms** related to box making and their use in this book is included. In addition, we list **Box Making Resources** that include books that offer helpful box making information, schools and organizations that offer workshops in box making, and a list of retail suppliers that carry many of the tools and materials needed. We also include an **Appendix**, listing conversions from fractions to decimals and from fractions to millimeters.

Three Tier Stacking Box with Ribbon Tab, 3 1/2" x 3 1/2" x 4".

This chapter covers the basic materials, tools, and supplies needed for box making. The most common materials include book board, book cloth, decorative paper, and PVA glue. The basic tools recommended include a cutting mat, light and heavy-duty cutting knives, ruler, glue brush, scissors, bone folder, and weights. Along with a few other supplies such as waste sheets, wax paper, and paper towels, there is not a lot more needed to get started making boxes. Although some of the materials, such as book board and book cloth are a little more difficult to pick up at a local art supply store, there are a number of on-line sources available for these supplies. (See our resource listing in the back of the book.) Most of the tools we suggest are fairly common or can be improvised. Under each item listed below, we give a brief description and include appropriate notes or observations as they apply to box making.

Basic Materials

Book Board

Book Board is sometimes referred to as binder's board and can be obtained in various grades. A standard quality, medium density board is recommended because it is fairly easy to cut with a utility knife. A higher quality book board, often known as Davey board, is more dense and sturdier. However, the drawback for the beginner is that Davey board is more difficult to cut.

Chipboard is sometimes used as a material for making boxes. Although it is somewhat less consistent in terms of quality, it can be an adequate substitute. Mat board can also be used. However, because it is relatively thin, two or more layers may need to be glued together to obtain the desired thickness.

Samples of book board ranging in thickness from 1/16" to 1/8".

Book board can be obtained in various thicknesses. We have found most to be in the range of 1/16" to 1/8" thick. It is more typical to see the thickness listed in thousands of an inch, such as .080. Book board we use is available in thicknesses of .060 (approximately 1/16"), .080 or .087 (both approximately 3/32"), and .098 (approximately 1/8").

The instructions and formulas in this book are based on the thickness of book board we use, approximately 3/32". Specifically, we use the slightly less dense, Standard Book Board with a thickness of .087, mainly because it is easier to cut by hand than Davey Board.

A utility knife with a sharp blade cuts book board cleanly. It should be used along with a metal ruler or cutting bar and a large cutting mat. Both the process of cutting book board and the consideration of grain direction are discussed in the next chapter.

Chapter 1
Materials and Tools

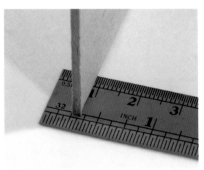

Book board with a thickness of .087 or approximately 3/32".

A swatch book from Hollander's shows the colors of Italian book cloth available.

Racks of decorative papers in Hollander's.

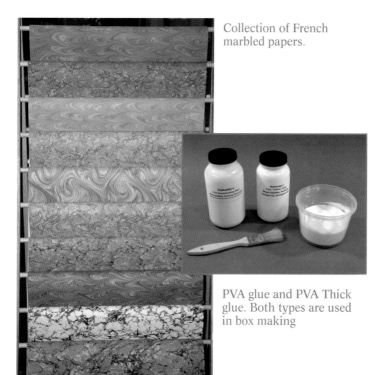

Collection of French marbled papers.

PVA glue and PVA Thick glue. Both types are used in box making

Book Cloth

Book cloth is a common covering material used in bookbinding and box making. Traditional book cloth is manufactured with a starch additive, which makes it non-porous and durable. Elegant paper-backed cloth, such as Japanese book cloth, has become more available recently.

Book cloth, because it is a stronger material than paper, is often used for covering the hinged area along the spine of a box. Since boxes are often opened and closed repeatedly like books, this strong material is preferable for the hinge. While most boxes use a combination of book cloth and decorative papers as covering materials, some boxes may be covered completely with book cloth.

Decorative Paper

Decorative paper offers countless possibilities in terms of color, texture, and design. Because of the wide array of decorative papers now available, covering a box is an exciting, creative experience. Although almost any paper can be used, we suggest that you do not use papers that are either too thin or too thick to work with.

Paper we refer to as "text" weight is an ideal thickness to use for covering the outside and inside of a box. Text papers have an approximate weight of the text pages in a book or of copy paper. Sometimes you will see the weights of text papers listed by a numerical weight, such as 70-pound text or 110 grams/square meter (70 lb or 110g/m^2). Typical text weight papers we like to use are marbled papers, various prints, and many of the decorative papers from Japan.

Inside the box, we might use either a contrasting or complementary solid color as a lining paper. One category of decorative papers that comes in a wide variety of colors is called Lokta. These handmade papers from Nepal, with their rich and almost leather-like texture, are ideal as solids used to line the inside of a box. Many other papers, including those that are textured, printed, marbled, or even solid colored art papers, can be used as a box lining.

Glues

The most widely used glue in most paper crafts today and one ideally suited for box making is called PVA, which is the abbreviation for polyvinyl acetate. This water soluble, white glue is specifically designed to maintain flexibility over time so that it does not become brittle after it dries. It is non-toxic and archival.

We recommend using PVA glue in two forms for box making. One of these we call simply PVA, which is the regular, thinner version. PVA pours a little like cream. As PVA is exposed to air, the water content begins to evaporate. Over time the glue will thicken up slightly and therefore, you may want to dilute it slightly and periodically with water. The desired consistency is a matter of preference, but using it straight out of the container when first purchased is usually fine.

The second form of PVA is a thick version which has a consistency similar to pudding. An advantage of using PVA Thick glue is that it dries quickly and enables you to easily attach the edges of the board together without the need of supports or tape to hold up the sides of the trays. PVA Thick glue is also used to attach the lid to the tray(s).

8

Basic Tools

Rulers, Squares, Cutting Bars, and Measuring Guides

A metal ruler is essential for measuring book board, paper, and book cloth. Several sizes ranging from 6" to 36" in length are good to have available, but a 12" and 24" are usually adequate. Make sure your ruler is marked in 1/16" increments. You can also use a ruler as a straight edge to cut against when cutting your materials.

A carpenter's square might also be helpful for assuring that book board and paper are cut square. A heavy, straight edge is another recommended tool. It will make cutting book board with a utility knife an easier process than using a lighter weight metal ruler.

Measuring or spacing guides are a great aid for quick and repeated measurements where consistency and accuracy are important. The most common one we use is a 3/16" spacer guide, used for measuring the gap that forms the hinge between the spine and lid boards. We make this guide using the thickness of two narrow pieces of .087 book board, glued together. Since the thickness of the board we commonly use is 3/32", the two edges glued together equals 3/16". Over time, you may find that a number of other guides and jigs are helpful to use for various measurements.

Cutting Mats

You must use a cutting mat or scrap board to protect your table top and knife blades. A large, self-healing cutting mat is an ideal surface for board and paper cutting, as well as a surface for working on. The larger the cutting mat, the better, and if room allows, we recommend one that is 24" x 36". Smaller ones may be used as well, but are not as functional, especially for cutting down larger sheets of board and paper. It is also helpful if the cutting mat has at least a 1/8" grid or markings to use as a guide for measuring and cutting. When used properly, the grid makes an adequate substitute for using a ruler. When laying your board or paper on the cutting mat, the grid enables you to make a cut without needing to mark the material with a pencil.

Cutting Knives

You will need a lightweight knife and a heavyweight knife for cutting. Typically, the lighter weight cutting knives such as a #1 or #2 X-acto knife work well for cutting paper and book cloth. For cutting book board, it is essential to use a heavier knife, such as a utility knife. Knives with break off blades offer the benefit of keeping your spare blades attached to the knife. Replace the blades frequently to assure the best and safest cutting results.

An assortment of rulers, cutting bars, and squares are helpful.

The 3/16" thickness of a guide stick made from gluing together two edges of .087 (3/32") board.

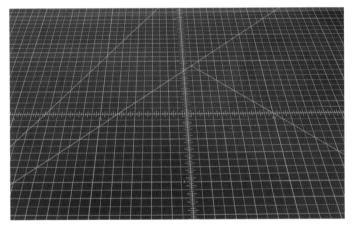

A large self healing cutting mat is essential for cutting materials on. Try to find one with at least 1/8" grid markings.

A utility knife for cutting book board and a light weight knife for cutting paper and book cloth are recommended. Make sure to have plenty of extra blades available.

A standard 6" bone folder is shown in the middle. The top folder is made from Teflon, which lessens the marring of paper when it is rubbed down. A mini bone folder is also shown.

Bone Folders

One of the most indispensable tools used in box making is a bone folder. It is commonly used by bookbinders, for folding and creasing, and a number of other functions. For box making it can be used for reaching into corners and pressing the paper down along the bottom inside edges. A bone folder can also be used for pressing the paper into the gap between the spine and lid.

Teflon folders are a recent adaptation that allows you to rub the folder over the surface of paper or book cloth without burnishing it, as you might with a bone folder.

We occasionally have used the flat edge of a 3" mini bone folder as a PVA Thick Glue Applicator and the pointed edge as a Scraper. (See Thick Glue Applicator and Scraper below.)

A good quality scissors with a sharp point is recommended.

Scissors

You will need a good quality, medium length scissors. As with any tool, the better the quality, the better the performance. We have used Wiss® bent handle scissors for years and have been extremely happy with their ability to miter corners and cut crisply through freshly glued paper. Scissors with a sharp point are desired.

It is helpful to have several sizes of good quality brushes.

Glue Brushes

Although almost any brush will work for gluing, those with stiffer (hog) bristles are best for use with PVA glue. A high quality brush is less likely to lose its bristles with repeated use and cleans up easier with water.

A 1" wide brush is adequate; however, it is helpful to have several sizes of brushes ranging from 1/4" up to 1 1/2". A round brush holds more glue than a flat brush, but either a round or flat brush works well. A brush with a very narrow width can be used to touch up a small area that needs to be glued or re-glued.

A Thick Glue Applicator (center) is used to apply PVA Thick Glue to edges of book board. A Thick Glue Scraper (top) is used to scrape away excess glue inside the tray. A mini bone folder may also be used.

Thick Glue Applicator/Scraper

You will need simple thick glue tools. The Thick Glue Applicator tool is one you can easily make using a piece of book board approximately 1/2" wide by 3" in length. The grain should run along the 3" length for increased strength. It is used to apply PVA Thick Glue to the edges of the book board when constructing a box. Its use is explained in Chapters 3 and 4.

The Thick Glue Scraper tool uses the same measurements and grain direction as the Thick Glue Applicator. However, at one end make a 45-degree angled cut with your scissors, leaving a small straight edge of 1/8" at the tip. A Scraper is used to scrape off excess Thick Glue that oozes out along the edges of the box as it is being constructed.

A 3" mini bone folder can be used as both an applicator and scraper tool.

Makeshift weights from covered bricks to shrink-wrapped packs of legal pads.

Weights

Weights are important to assure that book board dries flat, especially the lid, after paper or book cloth has been glued to it. Makeshift weights work fine, and almost anything that is compact and heavy can be used. We have used covered bricks, heavy books, shrink wrapped stacks of legal pads, cloth covered soft weights, and a number of other flat, heavy objects.

Basic Supplies

Wax Paper
Wax paper is primarily used during box construction. Wax paper allows for an easy release when picking up the tray after it has been glued.

Waste Sheets
Waste sheets are used to glue on and may also be referred to as scrap paper. We use blank newsprint, copy paper, or pages from old telephone books. Avoid using newspapers as waste sheets, because the ink may smudge onto your hands or materials.

Pencil
Use a pencil for marking book board, book cloth, and paper measurements as well as for labeling pieces after they are cut. Both a standard lead and a white pencil for marking on dark papers are useful.

Damp Wash Cloth and Paper Towels
Keep both a damp wash cloth and dry paper towels handy to wipe glue off your fingers. Be careful to place the damp cloth in a container that won't accidentally rest against your work in progress.

Optional Tools and Supplies

Micro Spatula
A micro spatula may be used for touching up a small unglued area or adding glue to a spot that a brush might not be able to reach, such as in the corner of a box. It may also be used for lifting glued paper off the waste sheet, keeping your fingers free of glue. We have occasionally used an X-acto knife in the same manner.

Wood Chisels
Standard size wood chisels are used to create a narrow slot in book board in order to feed various size ribbons through the lids for use as tie closures or tabs. Typical sizes of 3/8", 1/2", 5/8", and 7/8" are used, depending on the width of the ribbon. A heavy hammer is needed to strike the chisel. A piece of scrap board should be placed under the board when hammering.

Pressing Boards
Pressing boards are typically made of finished 3/4" plywood or 1/4" Plexiglas. We like to place a board over the lid of a box and add heavy weight on top to help assure that the lids dry flat. Usually it is best to allow a piece to dry overnight in this fashion.

Sand Paper
A piece of medium to fine grit sand paper can be used to lightly sand and smooth the edges and corners of a tray after construction.

A micro spatula is used for gluing tight areas that a brush may not reach.

Wood chisels are used to cut narrow slots in book board for ribbon tabs and tie closures.

Plywood or Plexiglas may be used as pressing boards in conjunction with a heavy weight.

11

An industrial strength glue gun may be used to glue trays to the lids instead of PVA Thick glue.

A good quality paper cutter can be used to cut paper and book cloth.

A board trimmer, such as this late nineteenth century 42" Jacques Board Shear, was designed specifically for cutting through thick book board.

Masking Tape

Masking tape is handy to have nearby. On occasion we will use it to hold the sides of the tray that have just been thick glued together, especially if they want to bow out from the piece you are attempting to glue it to. Once the glue dries, remove the tape.

Glue Gun

An industrial strength glue gun can be used to quickly glue the lid to the tray. Using a glue gun requires that you be extremely accurate because the glue dries almost instantly upon contact. If you decide to use a glue gun, we recommend using a high quality commercial grade model such as the 3M Polygun TC. Steer away from the inexpensive craft glue guns, as the glue is usually too weak to hold the larger boxes together for any length of time.

Paper Cutters

Most higher end model paper cutters are a worthwhile investment if you are going to do a lot of paper or book cloth cutting. Our favorite is the Ingento 30" Model. The blades on all the Ingento models are self-sharpening. Although a good paper cutter is great for cutting paper, never use a paper cutter to cut book board, as it is a sure way to ruin the blade and cutting mechanism.

Board Trimmer

Board trimmers or board shears are specifically designed for cutting book board. The best models are no longer being manufactured and the old ones are difficult to find. The one we use in our studio and workshops is a Jacques Board Shear, which was manufactured in the 1890s. Although there are some adequate quality board trimmers being manufactured today, there are none that we would highly recommend. All things considered, for the beginner we suggest using a utility knife, straight edge or cutting bar, and a large cutting mat.

Chapter 2
Basic Methods

In this chapter we consider some of the basic methods or techniques related to box making. These include determining grain direction, pattern layout, cutting materials, and gluing. We also include a number of helpful tips in this chapter.

Determining Grain Direction

It is possible to make a box paying absolutely no attention to grain direction. However, structurally, the strongest boxes will be made when you understand what is meant by "grain long" and "grain short." This is especially true when constructing a box using book board.

The grain direction of book board and paper is determined during its manufacturing process. As the pulp's fibers are pulled along a conveyor belt, most of the fibers align themselves in the direction in which the belt is moving. The parallel alignment of these fibers is what creates the grain. When the grain is running the length or the long direction of the material, we call it grain long. When the grain is running the width, or the short direction, we call it grain short.

Determining Grain Direction of Book Board

The simplest test for determining the grain direction of book board is to start with a larger piece of book board and gently bend it in both directions. The grain direction will run parallel to the direction that exhibits the least resistance. It is helpful to mark the grain direction directly on the board with an arrow.

Gently bend a large piece of book board to determine the grain direction. On this board, the grain runs long.

Be aware that the same size piece of book board can be either grain long or grain short, depending on how it is cut. For example, if you cut two pieces of book board at 2" x 8", one cut with the grain long, the other with grain short, the piece with grain long will be much stiffer and exhibit greater strength. The piece with grain long means that the grain runs long or parallel to the 8" length.

Narrow board piece with grain running long as indicated by the arrow. Note the relative resistance when trying to bend it.

13

The piece with grain short means that the grain runs short or parallel to the 2" width. In box making, you would want to use the stronger pieces, those with grain running long, for constructing the tray.

Board piece with grain running short as indicated by the arrow. Note how much easier it bends than the same size piece with the grain running long.

Note: As a general rule, when cutting book board, you will want to lay out all the pieces on the board so that the grain is long.

In most cases book board should be laid out with the graining running long.

The only exception to this rule is when making a lid for a box with a horizontal or landscape orientation. In this case the lid pieces should be arranged so that the grain is running parallel with the spine of the box. This means that the grain short direction applies only to the top and bottom lid pieces. (The spine piece will run long.) Other than this one exception, the grain of book board should always be cut grain long.

Box with a horizontal or landscape orientation whereby the grain runs parallel to the spine. This means that the grain direction of the top and bottom lid pieces runs short.

Determining Grain Direction of Papers

The same general rules for determining grain direction for book board apply to paper. However, with the wide variety of papers available today, determining grain direction may be a little more difficult. Western machine-made papers, such as the Florentine prints, have a very pronounced grain, whereas many Asian papers exhibit very little grain direction. Handmade papers exhibit virtually no grain direction.

The easiest and quickest way to determine the grain direction of paper is to bend the paper over on itself. Starting with a large sheet, lightly bend the paper in one direction. Notice the height of the bend as well as the resistance it offers. Next, bend the paper in the opposite direction. Note the difference in the height of the bend and the resistance you feel. The direction that exhibits the smallest bend or gives the least resistance is the grain direction of that sheet. In other words, as with book board, the grain runs parallel to the direction that exhibits the least resistance.

When testing for paper grain direction, first bend the paper over on itself in the long direction and note the height and resistance of the bend.

Next, bend the paper over on itself in the short direction and note the height and resistance of the bend. The less pronounced bend when folding the paper in the short direction means the grain runs short.

Another test for determining grain direction is to dampen the paper with a sponge. If the paper has a noticeable grain direction, the paper will begin to curl in the direction parallel to the grain. This is especially effective for determining the grain direction of a smaller piece of paper, where it might be difficult to see and feel the grain from bending it.

Another test for grain direction is to dampen the paper and note that the curl runs parallel to the grain of the paper.

You can also test for grain by tearing a small scrap piece of the paper. Paper will generally tear in a relatively smooth, straight line when torn along the grain. Against the grain, the tear line will be more uneven.

Book Cloth Grain Direction

To determine grain direction of book cloth we use a similar bending test as for paper. Grain direction of book cloth should also run the same direction as the grain direction of book board. More importantly, however, is that grain direction of book cloth should always run parallel to the grain direction of the spine of the lid. This allows for less resistance on the hinge as the lid is opened and closed repeatedly.

When determining the direction of most book cloth, follow the same basic test as you do for paper and note the resistance. Some book cloths have a paper backing. When testing for grain direction be sure to bend the book cloth over onto itself so that the paper backing is on the inside of the bend and the cloth on the outside. This allows you to test the grain of the paper, unencumbered by the cloth.

Drawing a pattern lightly on the back of a decorative paper in pencil.

Bend paper-backed book cloth over itself with the paper on the inside to get the correct read on grain direction.

An alternative and quicker cutting technique is to use the grid on a large cutting mat. This method will be explained in more detail in the cutting section in this chapter.

Breaking the Rule

A general rule regarding both pattern layout and grain direction is that the grain direction of book board and grain direction of the materials used to cover it, such as paper and book cloth, should line up together. In other words, if the grain of the book board runs long, the grain of the paper should also run long.

However, there are some exceptions. The most notable for us is when we are cutting a decorative paper that has a particular design that we want to orient in a certain direction on a box. For example, if your decorative paper is an image of a map that you want to position on the lid and the grain direction of the paper is the opposite of what the rule dictates, we will break the rule and position the paper in the direction it would look the most appropriate on the cover.

Pattern Layout

Measure Twice, Cut Once!

After determining the grain direction for all your materials, the next step is to measure and lay out patterns so that you can proceed to cut all the pieces. If you are making boxes for the first time, we recommend that you use the predetermined measurements as suggested at the beginning of Chapter 3 for the hinged lid box and Chapter 4 for the clamshell box. This will enable you to focus on the construction and covering techniques without the necessity of determining your own measurements.

After you have made a box, determining your own measurements by using the formulas in Chapter 6 will seem less complicated.

When laying out a pattern, attempt to be economical so that ultimately you are making as few cuts as possible. Sharing the edge of one piece with another of similar size will save you time measuring and cutting.

One easy method to lay out the pattern directly onto the materials is by using a sharp pencil and a ruler to mark the dimensions. Mark directly on the book board or the back of the paper and book cloth. You should also label each piece with a name and/or numbers as used in Chapters 3 and 4. This will be helpful in keeping your cut pieces organized so that you can more easily identify them.

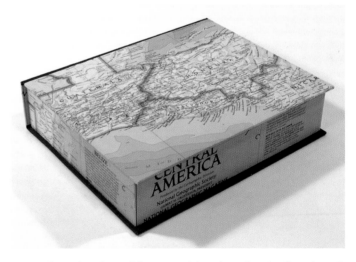

Map oriented on box without consideration of grain direction of paper, 8" x 10" x 2 1/4".

The concern with not matching the grain direction of both materials is that book board may have a tendency to warp slightly. In our experience, we have found this to be less of a problem than the theory behind it, especially if the lid is lined with an equal weight paper and is placed under a heavy weight to dry.

Cutting Materials

Cutting Book Board

For most people without access to commercial board cutting equipment, cutting book board is a significant challenge in box making because of the difficulty in cutting through the thickness of the board. For the price, the best tool we have found for cutting book board is a good quality utility knife with lots of new blades. You will also need a metal straight edge and a large cutting mat. In addition, a carpenter's square can be helpful to assure that the pieces are cut square.

To cut book board using a utility knife and metal straight edge, set yourself up at a sturdy table and position your board on a large cutting mat. You will want to stand while cutting. This will enable you to apply maximum pressure on the straight edge and keep it in a stable position. Cut with the blade pressed against the straight edge, using several long strokes with the knife. Stand slightly to the side as you bring the blade towards you.

Cutting book board using a heavy cutting bar, utility knife, and cutting mat.

Your first stroke should be the lightest. Gradually increase the pressure as you continue to cut through the board. Depending on the book board's thickness, the amount of pressure applied, and the sharpness of the blade, we have found that it will usually take from five to ten strokes to cut all the way through book board. Cut slightly beyond the end of the measurement in both directions to make a clean corner.

Throughout cutting, continue applying firm downward pressure on the straight edge as well as the knife. You should also be sure to keep sideways pressure against the metal straight edge to prevent the knife from slipping off line.

On long cuts and as the knife is being drawn towards you, it is helpful to stop and shift your fingers along the straight edge every so often. This allows you to maintain firm pressure along the entire length of the cut.

Do not rush your cutting. Rushing will result in either the metal edge shifting or the blade slipping off the line you are trying to cut. Be aware that cutting book board can be extremely dangerous and that the utmost precaution should be taken. Remember to replace the blades frequently for best cutting results and always properly dispose of the used blades.

We recommend that you do not attempt to cut book board on a paper cutter. It will not only ruin the blade as well as the hinge mechanism, but because it is not clamped down, the board will shift as it is being cut.

Cutting Decorative Paper and Book Cloth

You will quickly discover that cutting paper and book cloth with a lightweight knife is much easier than cutting book board with a utility knife. The same general format and technique described for cutting book board should be used for cutting paper and book cloth. The most notable difference is that decorative paper and book cloth will require only one or two passes to cut through the material.

A large cutting mat with a grid of 1/8" can be used effectively to eliminate the need to measure and mark a pattern on the back of the paper or book cloth. It also allows you to see the design of the paper as you are cutting, rather than cutting from a pattern that you have laid out on the backside. This is especially helpful if the piece you are cutting is somewhere in the middle of the paper.

To cut using the grid of a cutting mat, position the paper or book cloth so that two perpendicular edges are lined up on two perpendicular grid lines. Make sure the paper is perfectly square on the grid. Lay a metal straight edge across the paper or book cloth so that the ruled measurements on the cutting mat are visible on either side of the material before cutting.

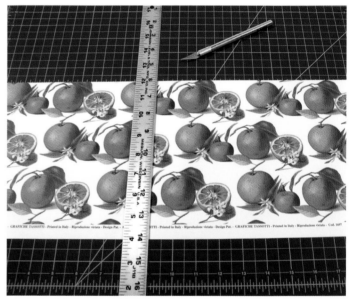

Cutting paper using the grid and rule of the cutting mat to align paper and the straight edge.

Always start by cutting your longest measurement first and continue working from the largest pieces to the smallest. Remember to check grain direction to assure that you are cutting the materials appropriately. After cutting each piece, be sure to identify the pieces in light pencil on the back.

If using a cutting mat with a 1/8" grid and you need to cut 1/16", split the difference on the grid. It is rare you will need to cut a measurement of less than 1/16".

Gluing

This section includes basic gluing techniques as well as a number of gluing tips.

Gluing Essentials

As described in Chapter 1, we recommend two types of glue for box making, PVA and PVA Thick glue. For gluing paper and book cloth to book board, PVA is an excellent adhesive. It spreads easily, dries quickly, and because it is water soluble, it is easy to clean up afterwards. We most often use it straight out of the container without needing to dilute it or mix it with other ingredients.

PVA used straight from the bottle and poured into a wider mouth container.

PVA glue may be diluted slightly with water to make it spread easier, especially as some of the water content evaporates from being exposed to the air over a period of time. PVA Thick glue, on the other hand, does not dilute easily with water. Once Thick glue begins to dry out, it is difficult to reconstitute.

On occasion the quick drying time of PVA may not be what you want, especially if you are gluing large pieces or need to reposition the paper. To lengthen the drying time, we mix a small amount of methyl cellulose with PVA. Methyl cellulose comes as a powder and is mixed with water.

Care in gluing should be taken because PVA is not very friendly when you accidentally get some glue on the "good" side of the paper or book cloth. Although it dries clear, it is difficult to remove and will often leave an unattractive dark spot.

In most cases you will want to glue onto a waste sheet. We often use newsprint, old copy paper, or cut out telephone pages. Remember to always remove and discard the waste sheet right after gluing, otherwise you are likely to set your work back on the glue.

When gluing, always brush evenly from the center out towards the edges. Hold the piece down firmly to prevent it from shifting while gluing. This will assure that you will not let the paper slip on the waste sheet and get glue on the "good" side.

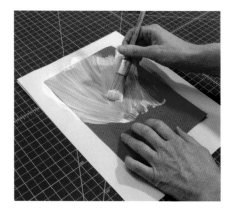

Spread glue from the center of the paper to the edges using a firm pressure to assure the paper does not slip on the waste sheet.

Preventing Wrinkles

As you are gluing, allowing the glue to soak into the paper for a few seconds will help the paper to stretch and relax. This will help prevent wrinkles in the paper if it is applied to the board too quickly after gluing. You will begin to notice that some papers curl up uncontrollably when glue is initially applied. This can be a problem, especially with many machine-made papers.

If you find that your paper curls excessively, use a damp cloth or sponge to coat the back of the paper, allowing the moisture to help stretch the fibers. When wetting the paper with a sponge, you will see the paper noticeably curl at first and then relax. Once you see the paper start to relax you can apply glue without worrying about it curling again.

Apply water with a sponge to relax the paper before gluing.

Paper curls up in response to moisture.

Paper relaxes after absorbing moisture.

After the paper is applied to the board, rub it down with your fingers or the palm of your hand. If you use a bone folder, it is a good idea to protect the surface with a clean sheet of paper so you do not mar the paper. We often use a Teflon folder, which will usually not burnish the paper if rubbed directly on the surface.

Since both unbacked and paper-backed book cloth does not stretch and relax the same way paper does, when book cloth is glued, curling can be a problem. We avoid this problem by applying glue to the book board first and then placing it on the book cloth. Note that this method will not work for applying glued book board directly onto decorative paper.

Gluing Large Papers

Gluing a large piece of paper is sometimes difficult because it can become limp after gluing. In order to manage a large glued piece, first lay the paper down on the book board with the fore edge of the paper towards the spine and the glued side up.

Then bring the front of the paper up over itself to glue in place along the spine. Next, reach under the glued edge and bring the paper out and towards the fore edge.

Re-Gluing and Touch Up

Sometimes as you are working, you will need to re-glue areas that might have dried or are close to drying. In these cases, there is a tendency to over glue. This can get messy, so when reapplying glue with a brush, make sure to apply only a very light coat.

If you miss gluing a small area, especially one that may be hard to reach with a brush, you can use a tool called a micro spatula to reach it. Place a very small amount of glue on the blade and slide it under the unglued area. We have also used an X-acto knife as a makeshift micro spatula for similar touch ups.

PVA Thick Glue

We have found PVA Thick Glue to be one of the best adhesives to use for constructing the trays. Thick glue is applied along the edges of the book board and is used to adhere the sides together and to the tray bottom. It dries quickly and is exceptionally strong.

Because PVA Thick glue is a fairly dense adhesive, we find that it is best applied using a stiff applicator, rather than a brush. An applicator can easily be made from thin board as described in Chapter 1.

A detailed explanation for applying thick glue to book board is described in Chapters 3 and 4 in the sections, **Constructing the Box Tray**.

Glue board first and then apply to book cloth.

To glue a large piece of paper, start with laying paper on the board with the glued side up.

Bring front of paper up and over itself to line up along spine.

Pull paper out from underneath and bring towards the fore edge.

Lay paper down on the lid.

Use a micro spatula for putting glue into tight spots.

Use PVA Thick glue to construct the box trays.

Use a PVA Thick Glue Applicator to apply Thick glue.

18

Chapter 3
Hinged Lid Box

Hinged Lid Boxes, 5 1/2" x 7 1/2" x 2", 8 1/2" x 11" x 3", and 10" x 13" x 2 1/2".

The first of the two basic styles of boxes described in this book is a hinged lid box. We suggest that the first box you attempt to make be based on the predetermined measurements listed below. This will give you an understanding of the techniques for making the box without concern over how to determine your own measurements. Afterwards, the chapter on formulas and how all the measurements are calculated will enable you to make your own custom size boxes.

Before following the step-by-step instructions in this chapter, it is helpful to review **Chapter 2 Basic Methods** for determining the grain direction of your materials, laying out your patterns, and cutting and gluing techniques and tips.

Part 1. Cutting and Labeling the Box Components

While you are cutting the materials, we suggest that you label the pieces. The corresponding names and/or numbers are used in the instructions to help you identify the parts. We have also listed the quantity of each piece that needs to be cut. To help with determining grain direction, we have underscored the measurement that denotes the long grain direction (ex. 7 1/2").

Book Board	Dimensions	Quantity
1. Lid	5 3/8" x 7 1/2"	(2)
2. Spine	1 13/16" x 7 1/2"	(1)
3. Tray Bottom	5" x 7"	(1)
4. Tray Long Side	1 3/4" x 7"	(2)
5. Tray Short Side	1 3/4" x 5 3/16"	(2)

Outside Paper		
6. Lid/Outside	6" x 9"	(2)
7. Spine/Outside	1 9/16" x 9"	(1)
8. Long Side/Outside	2 3/4" x 8 1/4"	(2)
9. Short Side/Outside	2 3/4" x 4 7/8"	(2)

Inside Paper		
10. Lid/Inside	5 1/8" x 7 1/8"	(1)
11. Long Side/Inside	1 3/4" x 6 7/8"	(2)
12. Short Side/Inside	1 3/4" x 5 1/2"	(2)
13. Bottom/Inside	4 7/8" x 6 7/8"	(1)

Book Cloth		
14. Spine/Outside	3 1/2" x 9"	(1)
15. Spine/Inside	3 1/2" x 7"	(1)

Part 2. Constructing the Box Tray

To assemble the box tray, you will need the following:

> Book Board Pieces: 3, 4, 5
> PVA Thick Glue
> Thick Glue Applicator
> Thick Glue Scraper
> Wax Paper

Step 1

Separate the box tray board pieces (3, 4, and 5 on the above list) from the lid pieces (1 and 2). The lid pieces will not be used in this section.

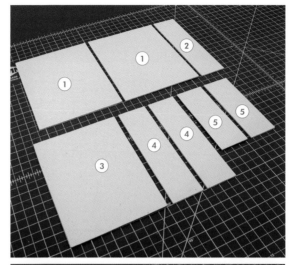

Cut book board pieces. The lid pieces are on the top. The tray pieces are on the bottom.

Step 2

Cut a piece of wax paper that is several inches larger than the box you will be constructing and lay out the five tray pieces.

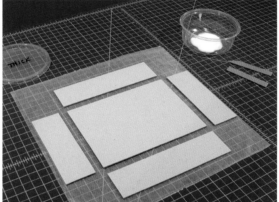

Book board pieces used for constructing the tray.

Step 3

Using the short straight edge of the Thick Glue Applicator, apply a small amount of thick glue to the four edges of the **Tray Bottom (3)**. Use a dabbing motion to create a uniform "bead" of glue along the edges, rather than a brushing motion.

Apply a bead of PVA Thick glue to all four edges of the Tray Bottom.

When applying the glue, try to avoid applying too much or too little. The right amount of glue should allow the thick glue to ooze just slightly after the tray sides are pressed into place along the edges of the Tray Bottom.

Note: After gluing all four edges, set the bottom down on the wax paper, working quickly enough to prevent the glue from drying. Generally, PVA Thick glue will begin to set in one to two minutes.

Tray Bottom placed on wax paper with all four sides having been glued.

Step 4

Apply PVA Thick glue, in the same manner as you did to the Tray Bottom, to both short edges of the two **Long Sides (4).**

Tray sides are sometimes referred to as walls.

Note: The two **Short Sides (5)** *will not* be glued.

Apply PVA Thick glue to both short edges of the two Long Sides.

Step 5

Place the **Long Sides (4)** against the long edges of the **Tray Bottom (3)** so that they are aligned evenly and hold them at a 90 degree angle for a few seconds.

The glue should be tacky enough that the sides should stay upright in that position after you release them.

Note: Gluing the tray sides against the edges of the tray bottom will give the sides more support than if the sides are glued on top of the tray bottom.

Place the Long Sides against the long edges of the Tray Bottom.

Step 6

Place the **Short Sides (5)** against the short edges of the **Bottom Tray (3)** so that they align with the glued edges of the **Long Sides (4)**. Push the ends of the Short Sides firmly against the edges of the Long Sides to assure good contact.

Note: The manner in which the tray sides are attached to the tray bottom and the adjoining sides is referred to as a butt joint.

Step 7

Take several moments to adjust the tray sides and tray bottom so that all the outside edges are flush. After carefully removing the tray from the wax paper, check the sides and bottom and make further adjustments if needed

Place the unglued Short Sides against the glued edges of the Long Sides.

Step 8

Use the Scraper tool or the pointed end of a bone folder to clean out any excess glue that has oozed inside the tray.

Step 9

Brush off any dried glue outside and inside the tray so that all the surfaces are smooth and make sure that all the sides and edges remain evenly aligned before setting the tray aside to dry.

Note: At this point, use a medium grit sand paper to smooth out any rough edges if necessary.

Use the Scraper tool to remove any excess thick glue from the inside of the tray.

Part 3. Covering the Lid

To cover the lid, you will need the following:

> Book Board: 1, 2
> Outside Papers: 6, 7
> Inside Paper: 10
> Book Cloth: 14, 15
> PVA Glue
> Waste Sheet
> Glue Brush
> Scissors
> Bone Folder
> 3/16" Spacer Guide
> Heavy Weight

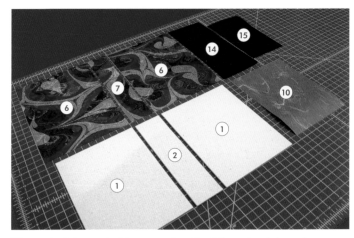

The materials needed for covering the lid are book board, decorative paper, and book cloth.

Step 1

Place several waste sheets on the table in front of you. Set the **Spine/Outside Book Cloth (14)** on the paper with the "wrong side" up. Pick up the **Spine/Board (2)** and apply PVA glue to one side of the piece.

Apply PVA glue to the Spine/Board.

Step 2

Center the spine on the book cloth so that the top, bottom, and sides are evenly spaced. You should see a margin of about 3/4" of book cloth along all four sides of the spine.

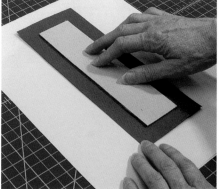

Center the Spine Board on the book cloth with a 3/4" margin or overlap on all four sides.

Step 3

Holding the **Spine/Board (2)** firmly on the waste sheet so that it does not shift while gluing, apply PVA along the margin of one long side of the book cloth. The other three sides do not need to be glued at this time.

Note: Be sure to remove and discard the waste sheet each time you glue so that you have a clean piece to work on.

Apply glue along one side of the book cloth.

Step 4

Insert the 3/16" Spacer Guides tight up to the **Spine/Board (2)** at the top and bottom of the spine. Allow the guide to extend off the book cloth to make it easier to remove. You can also use a ruler to measure the 3/16" gap.

Place 3/16" Spacer Guides along the top and bottom of the spine.

Step 5

Set one of the **Lid Boards (1)** onto the glued margin and snug to the spacer guide. The lid should be placed so that it is even across both the top and bottom of the spine.

Note: Remove the Spacer Guides quickly so they do not stick to the book cloth.

Place one Lid Board tight to the Spacer Guides and flush with spine at the top and bottom.

Step 6

Glue the remaining three margins of book cloth and place the second lid board on the opposite side of the spine in the same manner as in the preceding step.

Note: After a while you may be able to eye the spine gap without using a Spacer Guide or need to measure the gap with a ruler.

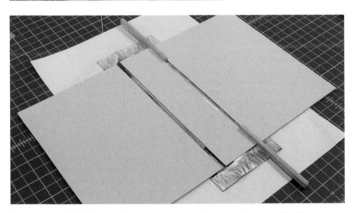

Set second Lid Board in place using the two Spacer Guides.

Step 7

Turn in the top and bottom margins, bringing the book cloth tight over the edges of the Spine and Lid Boards, and press down firmly. Use the bone folder to press the book cloth down into the gap between the spine and lid.

Turn the lid over, and using your thumb or the bone folder, lightly press the book cloth into the gap on the outside of the book cloth in the same manner as you did on the inside.

Turn in the book cloth at both the top and bottom of the spine and press down into the gap with the bone folder.

Use the bone folder on the outside of the spine to press into the gap.

Steps 8 and 9

Attaching the **Spine/Outside Paper (7)** is optional.

Decorative paper attached to the spine with 3/4" overlap for the turn-in.

Step 8

Glue the paper to the **Spine/Outside Book Cloth (14)**, allowing for a 3/4" overlap to turn in at the top and bottom. Center the paper on the spine, leaving an even margin of about 1/8" along the long edges on both sides of the **Spine/Board (2).**

Lid with decorative paper pressed down on the inside of the spine.

Step 9

Turn in the decorative paper onto the inside of the **Spine Board (2).**

Attach Spine Inside/Book Cloth along the inside of the spine, using the bone folder to press book cloth into the spine gap.

Step 10

Glue the **Spine Inside/Book Cloth (15)** onto the inside of the lid, centering it at the head and tail (top and bottom) and along the spine. Press down in the center of the spine first. Then press the book cloth into the gap between the lid boards and spine. Finally, press onto the lid boards.

This sequence helps secure the book cloth into the hinge gap before it gets pressed down onto the lid. Use firm pressure with the bone folder to press the cloth into the hinge.

Book cloth glued in place on the inside of the spine. Note the even spacing at the head and tail of the spine with the decorative paper just visible on the inside.

Step 11

Position the lid so that the bottom of the lid is on the table and the spine is upright with the top of the lid at an angle.

Prior to attaching the lid paper, set the lid so that the spine is in an upright position.

Step 12

Glue the **Lid/Outside Paper (6)** to the **Lid/Board (1).** Align the back edge or spine edge of the paper so that it is parallel with the spine and recessed approximately 1/8" from the spine edge of the lid board along the hinge.

When the paper is placed on the lid, you should note the 3/4" turn-in on both short sides, as well as along the fore edge.

Position the decorative paper so it is recessed 1/8" from the spine edge of the board.

Step 13

Turn the lid over so that you are now looking at it from the inside. With scissors, miter the two corners of the lid. These cuts should be made at a 45-degree angle, leaving a space of about 3/16" from the corner of the board. A properly mitered cut reduces the bulk at the corners when turning in the overlaps.

It might be helpful to use a ruler or the 3/16" spacer guide to help assure the accuracy of this cut. If the cut is too close, the corner will not be covered. If the cut is too far away from the corner, it looks bulky when turned in.

Note: As a general rule, the space between the corner and the cut is twice the thickness of the board.

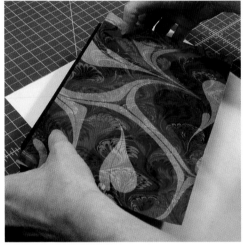

Miter the corner at a 45 degree angle.

Close-up showing a space of 3/16" between the corner and the cut. The distance is about twice the thickness of the board.

After turning in the short sides, tuck in the corners using the bone folder or a finger.

Step 14

Turn in the two short sides and press down onto the inside of the lid. Tuck in the paper, down and slightly inward, at each corner. Use a bone folder or the tip of your finger for this step.

Close-up of a neat tuck-in at the corner.

Step 15

Turn in the paper along the fore edge of the book board and press down onto the inside of the lid.

Step 16

Using the bone folder, tap the corners to help smooth or round any slight burr that might be present as a result of the turn-in.

Turn in the overlap at the fore edge and tap the corner with the bone folder.

Step 17

Repeat **Steps 11 through 16** to cover the other side of the lid in the same manner.

Lid from the inside after it has been covered with decorative papers.

Step 18

Select which side of the lid you want to be on the top when the box is closed and glue the **Inside Lid/ Paper (10)** to the inside of the lid you choose.

Note: The inside papers are sometimes referred to as the Lining.

When attaching the inside lining paper, leave an even margin of about 1/8" along the fore edge and along the two sides of the Lid/Board. We like to measure the spine edge of the paper to fit a little tighter, leaving only a 1/16" margin from the spine edge of the board.

There is no need to cover the bottom inside of the lid because the tray will be attached to it.

Inside decorative paper attached to inside top of the lid.

Step 19

When the lid is complete, place a heavy weight on it. It is helpful to use pressing boards or something solid before setting weights on top. Several large books are an adequate substitute for pressing boards and weights.

It is helpful to separate the pressing boards from the lid with a piece of wax paper to prevent any glue seepage from sticking to the boards.

Allow the lid to dry under heavy weight for at least several hours or overnight. This helps ensure the lid remains flat after it dries.

Place heavy weight on the lid and allow to dry.

Part 4. Covering the Tray

To cover the tray, you will need the following:

> Constructed (uncovered) Tray
> Outside Papers: 8, 9
> Inside Papers: 11, 12, 13
> PVA Glue
> Waste Sheets
> Glue Brush
> Scissors
> Bone Folder

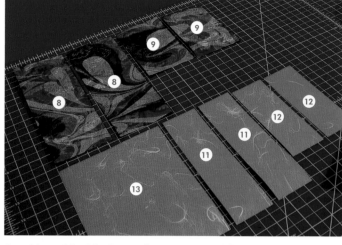

Outside and inside decorative papers used for covering the tray.

Step 1

Glue the **Long Side/Outside Paper (8)** and place on a waste sheet. Center the long side of the tray on the paper so that there is an equal overlap of approximately 1/2" along the two long sides and two short sides.

Align the long side of the tray on the Long Side paper allowing a 1/2" margin on all four sides.

Step 2

Wrap the paper around the corners of the tray so that both overlaps are glued onto the short sides. The corners of the paper will form a 90-degree angle above and below the sides of the tray. It is helpful to define these right angles by pinching them slightly with your thumb and fingers.

Wrap the paper around the side, forming 90 degree angles above and below the sides of the tray.

28

Step 3

Turn the tray over and miter the two corners on the bottom. Pointing your scissors from the outside towards the tray, miter each corner in a V-shape.

Note: Be sure to elevate the scissors slightly to assure you don't actually cut into the bottom corner of the tray.

Make a V-shape miter at the bottom of the tray.

V-shaped miter with cut completed.

Turn in the short tabs at both ends of the tray bottom.

Step 4

Turn in the short tabs created from the miter at each end of the tray and then turn in the long overlap along the length of the tray bottom.

Turn in the long overlap onto the tray bottom.

Step 5

Position the tray so that you are looking at the inside. Along the long side, and just to the inside of the corner, make a cut going straight down to the top edge of the board. The result of this cut will be a small tab.

Cut just to the inside of the corner along the long side of the tray creating a small tab.

Close-up of the cut that is just to the inside of the corner.

Press the tab inward and down so that it covers the inside corner of the tray.

Step 6

Press the tab created by the cut in Step 5 down onto the inside of the **Short Side/Board (5).** In the process, the tab will naturally twist and will cover the inside corner where the long and short sides meet.

Complete this step at both ends of the tray.

Tab shown covering the inside corner.

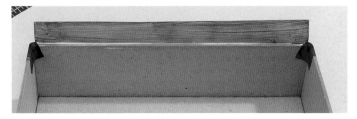

Turn in the overlap along the Long Side so that it fits neatly between the Short Sides.

Step 7

Turn in the long side overlap over the top edge of the **Long Side/Board (4)** and press down onto the inside wall of the tray.

As a result of the two cuts in Step 5, the turn-in will fit neatly between the **Short Side/Board (5)** without overlapping onto the Short Sides. When the turn-in is completed, the two inside corners should appear seamless.

Completed turn-in with paper pressed down onto the inside wall of the Long Side.

Step 8

Use the bone folder to tap the corners and help to smooth out any burrs or wrinkles. You can also use the bone folder on the inside of the tray to make sure the paper is pressed down tightly along the inside corners.

Use the bone folder to tap the corners and smooth out any wrinkles.

Step 9

Repeat **Steps 1 through 8** to glue the other Long Side of the tray.

Tray with both Long Sides glued in place.

Step 10

Glue the **Short Side/Outside Paper (9)** between the two long sides, centered so that there is a 1/2" overlap above and below the tray. It should also be recessed approximately 1/8" from the outside edges of the long sides.

Glue the Short Side so that it is centered approximately 1/8" from the outside edges of the Long Sides.

Step 11

Turn in the overlaps so that they are glued down to the outside bottom of the tray as well as over the top edge and onto the inside wall of the tray.

No cuts are necessary in this step because this piece has been measured to fit just to the inside of the long sides of the tray.

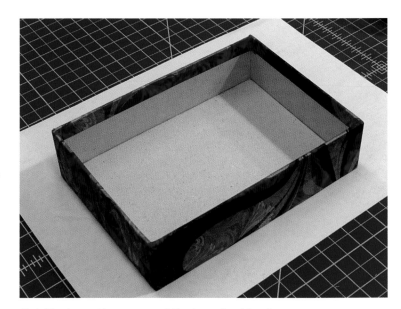

Outside decorative papers of the tray glued in place.

Step 12

Glue the **Short Side/Inside Paper (12)** to the **Short Side/Board (5).** When placing in position, recess the paper 1/8" from the top edge of the tray and allow for an equal amount (1/8") of overlap onto each long side, as well as onto the tray bottom.

Note: We deliberately make the margin of overlap narrow to reduce the bulk in the corners of the tray.

Use the bone folder to assist in pressing the paper tightly into the corners and along the bottom of the tray. Complete this step on both short sides.

Glue the Short Side/Inside Paper onto the Short Side of the interior of the tray.

Step 13

Glue both pieces of the **Long Side/Inside Paper (11)** into place. They should be recessed 1/8" from the top edge of the sides so that they line up with the same amount that the **Short Side/Inside Papers (12)** were recessed. Both pieces will fit neatly between the Short Sides with no overlap.

Glue the Long Side/Inside Paper onto the Long Sides of the interior of the tray.

Step 14

Glue the **Bottom/Inside Paper (13)** to the bottom of the tray. Once in place, use the bone folder to assist in pressing the paper down into the corners and along the four edges.

Glue the Bottom/Inside Paper for the tray bottom in place.

Part 5. Attaching the Tray to the Lid

To attach the tray to the lid, you will need the following:

> Completed Lid
> Completed Tray
> PVA Thick Glue
> Thick Glue Applicator
> Thick Glue Scraper
> Heavy Weights

Step 1

Check the fit of the tray and the lid. Select which long side of the tray you want as the "back." This side should be placed against the spine with the lid in the closed position.

With the tray set in place as if it was glued to the lid, check to make sure the lid closes properly. In addition, examine the margin along the short sides and front of the box. With the back of the tray sitting flush to the spine, the tray should have an equal margin or overhang of approximately 1/8" along the two short sides and the fore edge.

Note: The margin between the sides of the tray and the three edges of the lid is also known as the square.

The tray should have an equal margin or overhang of approximately 1/8" along the two short sides and the fore edge.

Step 2

Remove the tray and lay the lid flat. Apply a fairly generous bead of PVA Thick glue along the middle of the spine, using the Thick Glue Applicator.

Note: Be careful to apply the glue only on the center of the spine and not too close to the edges. When attaching the spine to the back of the tray, this allows for some oozing in all directions as pressure is applied.

Apply a fair amount of thick glue, centered on the spine.

Step 3

Place the tray on the bottom of the lid with a small weight inside for stability and to prevent shifting. Check to see that the margin or square of the tray and the edges of the lid remain at an equal distance of approximately 1/8" along the three sides.

Bring the spine up towards the outside back of the tray and apply moderate pressure between the outside of the spine and the inside back of the tray, drawing the two together. Hold the lid and tray in this position for about 30 seconds to allow the thick glue to set.

Bring the spine up to meet the outside back of the tray.

Step 4

Place the box upright and on its spine with the lid open and flat on the table. Be careful not to allow the tray to shift during this step.

Place a weight(s) to hold the tray securely along the length of the spine and allow to dry for at least 10 minutes.

Place tray upright with weights along the spine edge and allow to dry for at least 10 minutes.

Step 5

With the tray still in this upright position, apply PVA Thick glue to the inside bottom lid.

Recess the glue approximately 1/2" from the lid's three edges to allow for oozing when the tray is pressed down onto the bottom lid.

Apply thick glue to the bottom of the tray.

Step 6

Remove the weights from the spine and bring the tray down and onto the bottom lid and press firmly. Make sure that the margin along the three sides remains even.

Close the box onto the bottom of the tray.

Step 7

Once the tray is in position on the bottom lid, add weight to the interior of the tray. The more weight that is evenly dispersed within the tray the better.

If some glue oozes out along the bottom of the tray during this step, use the Thick Glue Scraper to remove it.

Add weights to the interior of the tray after gluing.

Step 8

With the box closed, place a heavy weight on top and allow the box to dry overnight. The heavy weight helps to secure the tray firmly to the lid as well as help the lid to dry flat.

Using pressing boards is optional.

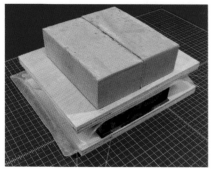

Box drying under pressing boards and heavy weights.

Completed Hinged Lid Box.

The second of the two basic types of boxes described in this book is the clamshell box, also called a two-tray drop spine box or portfolio box. Many of the techniques for constructing and covering the clamshell style are similar to the hinged lid box. However, there are some major differences. One of these is the technique for covering the open edge of a three-sided tray. Another major difference is that the trays are attached to both top and bottom lids. This allows for the spine to "drop" and for the box to lay flat when it is open.

As an alternative method for covering a tray, in this chapter we give instructions on how to use a single piece to cover the outside and inside of the tray. In addition, we introduce a different technique for covering the inside corners of a tray.

As with the hinged lid box, we suggest that the first box you attempt to make be based on the predetermined measurements listed below. This will give you an understanding of the techniques for making the box without concern over how to determine your own measurements. Afterwards, the chapter on formulas and how all the measurements are calculated will enable you to make your own custom size boxes, including a clamshell box to hold a book.

Before following the step-by-step instructions in this chapter, it is helpful to review Chapter 2 Basic Methods, for determining the grain direction of your materials, laying out your patterns, and cutting and gluing techniques and tips.

Chapter 4
Clamshell Box

Clamshell Boxes, 6 3/4" x 8 1/2" x 1 1/2" and 10" x 12 1/2" x 1 1/2".

Part 1. Cutting and Labeling the Box Components

While you are cutting the materials, we suggest that you label the pieces. The corresponding names and/or numbers are used in the instructions to help you identify the parts. We have also listed the quantity of each piece that needs to be cut. To help with determining grain direction we have underscored the measurement that denotes the long grain direction (ex. 8 3/8").

Book Board	Dimensions	Quantity
1. Lid	6 9/16" x 8 3/8"	(2)
2. Spine	1 5/16" x 8 3/8"	(1)
3. Small Tray Bottom	6" x 7 1/2"	(1)
4. Small Tray Long Side	1 1/16" x 7 11/16"	(1)
5. Small Tray Short Side	1 1/16" x 6"	(2)
6. Large Tray Bottom	6 1/4" x 7 7/8"	(1)
7. Large Tray Long Side	1 1/4" x 8 1/16"	(1)
8. Large Tray Short Side	1 1/4" x 6 1/4"	(2)

Paper

9. Lid	7 1/4" x 9 7/8"	(2)
10. Small Tray Long Side	3" x 8 3/4"	(1)
11. Small Tray Short Side	3" x 6 3/4"	(2)
12. Small Tray Bottom	6 3/4" x 7 3/8"	(1)
13. Large Tray Long Side	3 3/8" x 9"	(1)
14. Large Tray Short Side	3 3/8" x 7"	(2)
15. Large Tray Bottom	7" x 7 3/4"	(1)

Book Cloth

16. Spine/Outside	3 1/8" x 9 7/8"	(1)
17. Spine/Inside	3 1/8" x 7 9/16"	(1)

Part 2. Constructing the Box Trays

To assemble the box tray, you will need the following:

> Book Board Pieces: 3, 4, 5, 6, 7, 8
> PVA Thick Glue
> Thick Glue Applicator
> Thick Glue Scraper
> Wax Paper

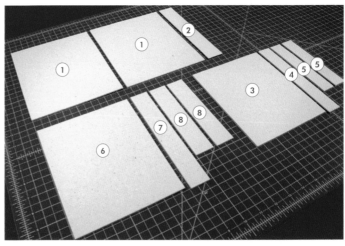

Step 1

Separate the tray board pieces into two sets, including the small tray (3, 4, and 5) and large tray (6, 7, and 8). The lid pieces (1 and 2) will not be used in this section.

Board pieces used for the clamshell box. Top pieces are used for the lid. Bottom pieces are for the large and small trays.

Step 2

Cut a piece of wax paper that is several inches larger than the box you will be constructing and lay out the board pieces for the small tray.

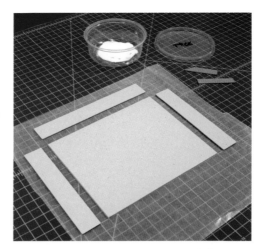

Book board pieces used for constructing the small tray.

Step 3

Using the short straight edge of the Thick Glue Applicator, apply a small amount of PVA Thick glue along the two short edges and one long edge of the **Small Tray/Bottom (3)**. Use a dabbing motion to create a uniform "bead" of glue along the three edges, rather than brushing it on.

When applying the glue, try to avoid applying too much or too little glue. The right amount of glue should allow the thick glue to ooze just slightly after the tray sides are pressed into place along the edges of the tray bottom.

After gluing the three edges, set the small tray bottom down on the wax paper, working quickly enough to prevent the thick glue from drying.

Apply a bead of PVA Thick glue to the two short and one long edge of the Small Tray/Bottom.

Step 4

Apply thick glue in the same manner to *only one* short edge of each of the **Short Sides (5)**.

Note: The **Long Side (4)** *will not* be glued.

Apply PVA Thick glue to only one short edge of both short sides.

Step 5

Place the **Short Sides (5)** against the short edges of the **Tray Bottom (3)** so that they are aligned evenly. The edge of the Short Side with PVA Thick glue should be facing in the same direction as the long edge of the Tray Bottom that also has Thick glue.

Hold the sides in place at a 90 degree angle for a few seconds. The glue should be tacky enough that the sides will stay upright in that position after you release them.

Place the Short Sides against the short edges of the Tray Bottom.

Step 6

Place the **Long Side (4)** along the glued long edge of the **Tray Bottom (3)** so that it meets the glued edges of the **Short Sides (5)**. Push the ends of the short sides firmly against the edges of the long side to ensure good contact.

Place the unglued Long Side in position against the glued short sides.

Step 7

Take several moments to adjust the tray sides and tray bottom so that all the outside edges are flush. After carefully removing the tray from the wax paper, check the sides and bottom and make further adjustments if needed.

Use the Thick Glue Scraper tool or the pointed end of a bone folder to clean out any excess glue that has oozed inside the tray.

Scrape any excess glue off the inside of the tray.

Step 8

Brush off any dried glue outside and inside the tray so that all the surfaces are smooth. Make sure that all the sides and edges remain evenly aligned before setting the tray aside to dry.

Step 9

Repeat Steps 3 through 8 with the Large Tray board pieces.

Step 10

Before proceeding, set the small tray inside the large and check the amount of space between the sides of each tray. The amount should be about 1/8". It should also be recessed from the top edge of the large tray by about 1/8". Covering the trays with decorative paper will add some thickness, so this extra space is desired. If the fit is any closer, the box may not close properly once both trays are covered.

Completed Small and Large Trays.

Part 3. Covering the Lid

The instructions for covering the lid of the clamshell box are basically the same as for the hinged lid box in the previous chapter. They are repeated here for the sake of continuity with the correct corresponding numbers for the clamshell box. The major difference is that the inside lining paper will not be attached, since it is not necessary. Also, the step for adding a decorative paper along the spine is omitted.

To cover the lid you will need the following:

> Book Board: 1, 2
> Outside Papers: 9
> Book Cloth: 16, 17
> PVA Glue
> Waste Sheets
> Glue Brush
> Scissors
> Bone Folder
> 3/16" Spacer Guide
> Heavy Weight

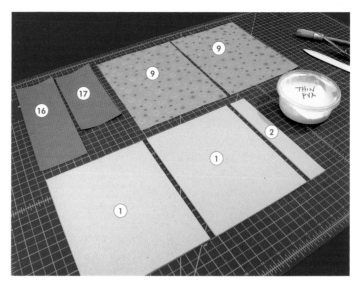

The materials needed for covering the lid are book board, decorative paper, and book cloth.

Step 1

Place several waste sheets on the table in front of you. Set the **Spine/Outside Book Cloth (16)** on the paper with the "wrong side" up. Pick up the **Spine/Board (2)** and apply PVA glue to one side of the piece.

Apply PVA thin glue to the spine board.

Step 2

Center the spine board on the book cloth so that the top, bottom, and sides are evenly spaced. You should see a margin of about 3/4" of book cloth on all four sides of the spine.

Center the spine on the book cloth with a 3/4" margin or overlap on all sides.

Step 3

Holding the **Spine/Board (2)** firmly on a waste sheet so that it does not shift while gluing, apply PVA along the margin of one long side of the book cloth. The other three sides do not need to be glued at this time.

Note: Be sure to remove and discard the waste sheet each time you glue so that you have a clean piece to work on.

Apply PVA along one edge of the book cloth.

Step 4

Insert the 3/16" spacer guides tight up to the **Spine/Board (2)** at both the top and bottom of the spine. Allow the guide to extend off the book cloth to make it easier to remove. You can also use a ruler to measure the 3/16" gap.

Place a 3/16" Spacer Guide along top and bottom of the spine.

Step 5

Set one of the **Lid Boards (1)** onto the glued margin and snug to the spacer guide. The lid should be placed so that it is even across both the top and bottom of the spine.
Note: Remove the Spacer Guides quickly so they do not stick to the book cloth.

Place one Lid Board tight to the Spacer Guides and flush with spine at the top and bottom.

Step 6

Glue the remaining three margins of the book cloth and place the second lid board on the opposite side of the spine in the same manner as in the preceding step.
Note: After a while you should be able to eye the spine gap without using a Spacer Guide or measuring the gap with a ruler.

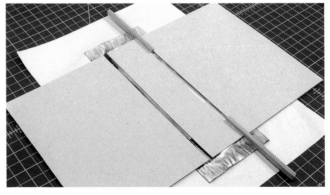

Set the second Lid Board in place using the two Spacer Guides.

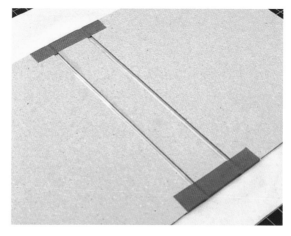

Turn in the book cloth at both top and bottom of the spine and press down into the gap with the bone folder.

Step 7

Turn in the top and bottom margins, bringing the book cloth tightly over the edges of the spine and lid boards and press down firmly. Use the bone folder to assist in pressing the book cloth down into the gap between the spine and lid.

Turn the lid over and using your thumb or the bone folder, lightly press the book cloth into the gap on the outside of the book cloth in the same manner as you did on the inside.

Use the bone folder on the outside of the spine to help press the book cloth into the gap.

Step 8

Glue the **Spine Inside/Book Cloth (17)** onto the inside of the lid, centering it top, bottom, and along the spine. Press down in the center of the spine first; then press the book cloth into the hinge, and finally press onto the lid boards.

This sequence helps secure the book cloth into the hinge, before it gets pressed down onto the lid. It is helpful to use the bone folder to press the book cloth into the hinge.

Attach book cloth to the inside of spine, pressing into the spine gap.

Step 9

Position the lid so that the bottom of the lid is on the table and the spine is upright with the top of the lid at an angle as shown.

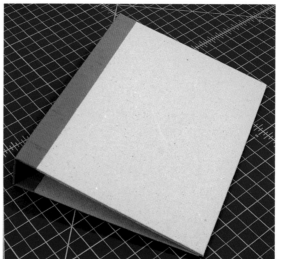

Place the lid in an upright position prior to attaching the lid paper.

Step 10

Glue the **Lid/Outside Paper (9)** to the **Lid/Board (1)**. Align the back edge of the paper so that it is parallel with the spine and recessed approximately 1/8" from the spine edge of the lid board along the hinge.

Place the paper on the lid so that you allow for a 3/4" turn-in on both short sides, as well as along the fore edge of the lid.

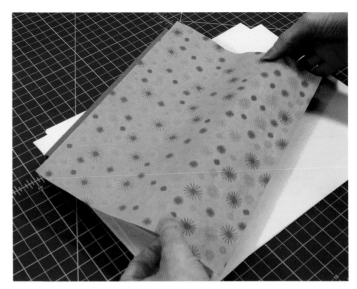

Position the decorative paper recessed 1/8" from the spine.

Step 11

Turn the lid over so that you are now looking at it from the inside. With scissors, miter the two corners of the lid. These cuts should be made at a 45-degree angle, leaving a space of about 3/16" from the corner of the board. A proper miter reduces the bulk at the corners when turning in the overlaps.

It might be helpful to use a ruler or the 3/16" spacer guide to help assure the accuracy of this cut. If the cut is too close, the corner will not be covered. If the cut is too far away from the corner, it looks bulky when turned in.

As a general rule, the space between the corner and the cut should be twice the thickness of the board.

Miter the corner at a 45 degree angle.

Close-up showing a space of 3/16" between the corner and the cut.

Step 12

Turn in the two short sides and press down onto the inside of the lid. Tuck in the paper, down and slightly inward, at each corner. Use a bone folder or the tip of your finger during this step.

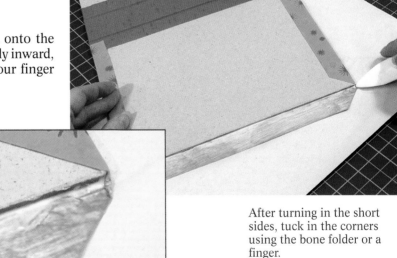

Close-up of a neat tuck-in at the corner.

After turning in the short sides, tuck in the corners using the bone folder or a finger.

Step 13

Turn in the paper at the fore edge of the board and press down onto the inside of the lid.

Turn in and glue down the margin along the fore edge.

Step 14

Tap the corners with the bone folder to help smooth or round any slight burr that might be present as a result of the turn-in.

Tap the corner with the bone folder to smooth.

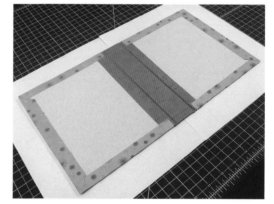

Completed lid from the inside after it has been covered with decorative papers.

Step 15

Repeat **Steps 9 through 14** to cover the other side of the lid.

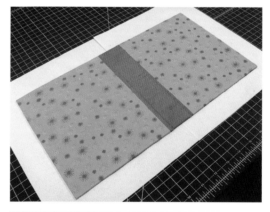

Completed lid from the outside after it has been covered with decorative papers.

Step 16

When lid is complete, place a heavy weight on it. It is helpful to use pressing boards or something solid before setting the weight on top. Several large books are an adequate substitute for pressing boards and weights.

It is helpful to separate the pressing boards from the lid with wax paper to prevent any glue seepage from sticking to the boards.

Allow the lid to dry under heavy weight for at least several hours or overnight. This helps ensure the lid remains flat after it dries.

Place heavy weight on the lid and allow to dry.

Part 4. Covering the Trays

To cover the trays, you will need the following:

Constructed Trays
Decorative Papers: 10, 11, 12, 13, 14, 15
PVA Glue
Waste Sheets
Glue Brush
Scissors
Bone Folder

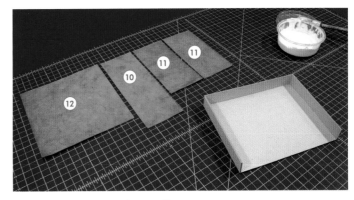

Papers used to cover the small tray.

Align the long side of the tray on the Long Side paper allowing 1/2" turn-ins on the bottom and along the two short sides.

Step 1

Glue the **Long Side/Small Tray Paper (10)** and place on a clean waste sheet. Pick up the tray and center it on the paper so that there is an equal margin of about 1/2" along the bottom of the tray and overlapping the two short sides.

However, because we are covering both the outside and inside of the tray with one piece, leave a 1 1/2" margin for the turn-in, which will be used to cover the inside of the tray.

Allow a 1 1/2" turn-in to cover the inside of the long tray side.

Step 2

Wrap the paper around the corners so that both 1/2" turn-ins are glued onto the short sides. After this is done, the corners of the paper will form a 90-degree angle above and below the sides of the tray. It is helpful to pinch the corners slightly, to help define the right angles.

Wrap the 1/2" margin around the side of the box forming 90 degree angles above and below the sides of the tray.

Step 3

Turn the tray over and miter the two corners on the bottom. Bring your scissors in from the outside and cut a V-shape from the paper at each corner. Elevate the scissors slightly to assure you don't cut into the bottom corners of the tray.

Make a V-shape miter cut on the bottom of the tray at both corners.

V-shaped miter after the cut is made.

Turn in the short tab onto the tray bottom at each corner.

Step 4

Turn in the short tabs first and then turn in the overlap along the bottom of the tray.

Turn in the overlap along the tray bottom.

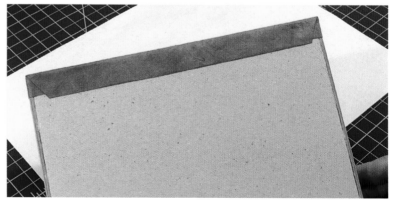

Step 5

Position the tray so that you are looking down at the inside corner. From the top, make two cuts straight down to the edge of the board at each corner. One cut will be along the long side and the other along the short side. The cuts to either side will form a narrow center tab that will be used to cover the corner.

Make two cuts on either side of the corner to form a narrow center tab.

Step 6

Carefully bring the narrow center tab down into the corner so that it just overlaps onto the **Long Side (4) and Short Side (5)** and onto the bottom of the tray. Complete this step at both corners of the long side of the tray.

Center tab shown covering the corner and overlapping onto the tray bottom.

Step 7

Turn in the two short tabs along the **Short Side/Board (5)** and press down onto bottom of the tray. The short side tab will align itself with the corner and overlap the narrow center tab.

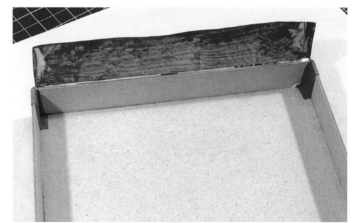

Turn in the Short Side tabs to cover the narrow center tab.

Turn in the Long Side overlap so that it fits neatly between the short sides.

Corners covered and turn-ins completed along the long side.

Step 8

Turn in the long side overlap, which will align itself with the corner and overlap the narrow center tab.

Throughout these steps, use the bone folder to assist in pressing the paper into the corners and along the edges.

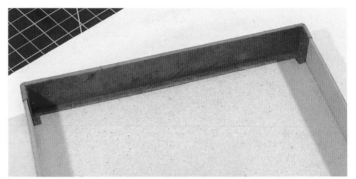

Step 9

Glue the **Short Side/Small Tray Paper (11)** to one of the tray's short sides. This piece should be placed so that it is recessed 1/8" from the long side. The overlap on the bottom should be about 1/2" below the tray. In addition, the paper should have an overlap at the top edge of the tray of 1 1/2" for the turn-in, as it did with the long side.

Tray with Short Side paper glued in place.

Step 10

Turn in the 1/2" overlap onto the bottom of the tray as you did with the Long Side in Step 4.

Turn in Short Side paper onto the bottom of the tray.

Step 11

Form a more defined 90 degree angle using your thumb and finger, which is important for the next series of cuts.

Note: Steps 12 through 14 will take you through a series of three cuts that will enable you to cover the open edges of the short sides of the tray.

Form a 90 degree angle using your fingers.

Step 12

Position the tray so that the open end is facing you. Cut 1 is made towards the front edge of the Short Side, just above the bottom of the tray. This will create a small tab that will cover the corner between the Tray Bottom and the Short Side.

Cut 1 is to the front edge of the Short Side, just above the bottom of the tray.

Step 13

Reposition the tray so that for Cut 2, you are cutting towards the tray from the top edge. Recess the cut approximately 1/16" from the front edge of the Short Side.

Note: It is important *not* to make this cut all the way to the board, but to stop 1/8" from the top edge of the tray side.

Cut 2 is from the top and is recessed 1/16" from the front edge of the Short Side. This cut should also stop 1/8" before the top edge of the board.

Step 14

Reposition the tray once again for Cut 3. This cut will be made on a diagonal, starting from the outside and meeting at the end point of Cut 2.

The cut will produce a second tab that will cover the front edge of the tray and allow the turn-in to fit neatly inside the front edge of the Short Side.

Cut 3 is a diagonal cut to meet the point where Cut 2 ended.

All three cuts completed showing two tabs and the piece that was cut out.

Step 15

Turn in the short tab created from Cut 1. Press the tab over the front edge of the Tray Bottom and so that it twists slightly and covers both the Tray Bottom and just onto the inside wall of the Short Side.

You may want to use the bone folder to help press the tab tightly into the corner.

Turn in the first tab created from Cut 1 to cover the front edge of the Tray Bottom and just onto the inside wall of the Short Side.

Step 16

Turn in the second tab to cover the front edge of the Short Side. This piece will cover the tab along the inside of the tray and fit neatly along the bottom.

Turn in the second tab from Cut 3 to cover the front edge of the tray.

Step 17

At the corner, where Cuts 2 and 3 met, tuck in the paper using the bone folder or the end of your finger.

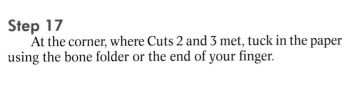

Tuck the corner inward slightly.

Step 18

Turn in the Short Side overlap and press down onto the inside of the tray. Use the bone folder to assist in pressing the paper along the bottom of the tray.

Turn in the Short Side overlap and press down to cover the inside wall and onto the Tray Bottom.

Step 19

Repeat **Steps 9 through 18** to complete the other Short Side of the Small Tray.

Use the bone folder to help press the paper down along the edges and smooth the corners.

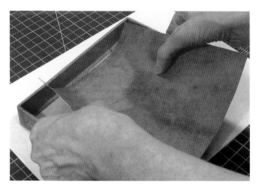

Glue the Bottom paper of the tray in place.

Step 20

Glue the **Small Tray/Inside Paper Bottom (12)** to the bottom of the tray. The paper should be placed evenly at the back of the tray and then brought tightly over the front edge and onto the under side of the tray.

Use the bone folder to press the paper down tightly along the edges of the tray bottom.

Bring the Bottom paper over the front edge and on to the under side of the tray.

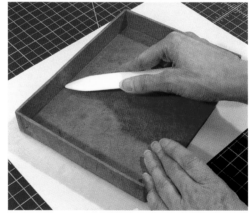

Press the paper down along the edges of the tray bottom with the bone folder.

Step 21

Repeat **Steps 1 through 20** to complete the large tray in the same manner as the small tray.

Part 5. Attaching the Trays to the Lid

To attach the trays to the lid, you will need the following:

> Completed Lid
> Completed Trays
> PVA Thick Glue
> Thick Glue Applicator
> Thick Glue Scraper
> Heavy Weights

Step 1

Decide which side of the lid you want to use for the top and bottom. Write "top" on the inside of the lid and "bottom" on the bottom.

It is important to make sure that the large tray is glued to the top lid and the small tray to the bottom, so you should also write "top" and "bottom" on the bottom of the large tray and small trays to be sure they are matched correctly.

Label the lid and trays with top and bottom to assure they match.

To get an idea of how the trays will be glued onto the lids, position both trays on the lid so that the open sides are placed towards the spine. The front of the open side of the trays should be lined up evenly with the spine edge of the lid board.

The trays should also be evenly recessed along the other three sides of the lid, with the larger tray having a smaller square or margin than the smaller tray.

Position the trays prior to gluing. Note the square of the large tray is smaller than the square of the small tray.

Step 2

Using the Thick Glue Applicator, apply a fairly generous bead of PVA Thick glue to the bottom of the small tray. Recess the glue approximately 1/2" from the bottom of the tray to allow for oozing when the tray is pressed down onto the bottom lid. Add some glue to the middle of the tray bottom as well.

Note: Unlike the hinged lid box, where we applied Thick glue to the lid and spine, with the clamshell box we apply Thick glue only to the bottom of the trays. Because the trays are two different sizes, this assures that the glue is applied in the correct position on the tray bottoms.

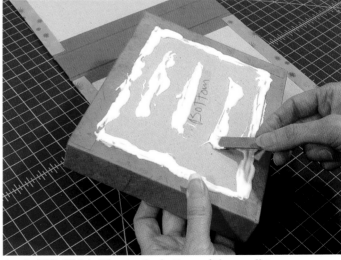

Apply PVA Thick Glue to the bottom of the small tray.

Press the small tray into position so that the edge of the open side is flush with the spine edge of the lid board.

Place heavy weights on the tray bottom.

Step 3

Carefully press the small tray into position with the open end facing the spine and lined up flush to the spine edge of the lid. The margin around the three outside edges should be even.

Add weight to the interior of the tray. The more weight that is evenly dispersed within the tray the better.

If some glue oozes out along the bottom of the tray during this step, use the Glue Scraper to remove it.

Step 4

Glue and attach the large tray in the same manner as the small tray.

Step 5

Check to make sure the trays have not shifted position and let dry overnight.

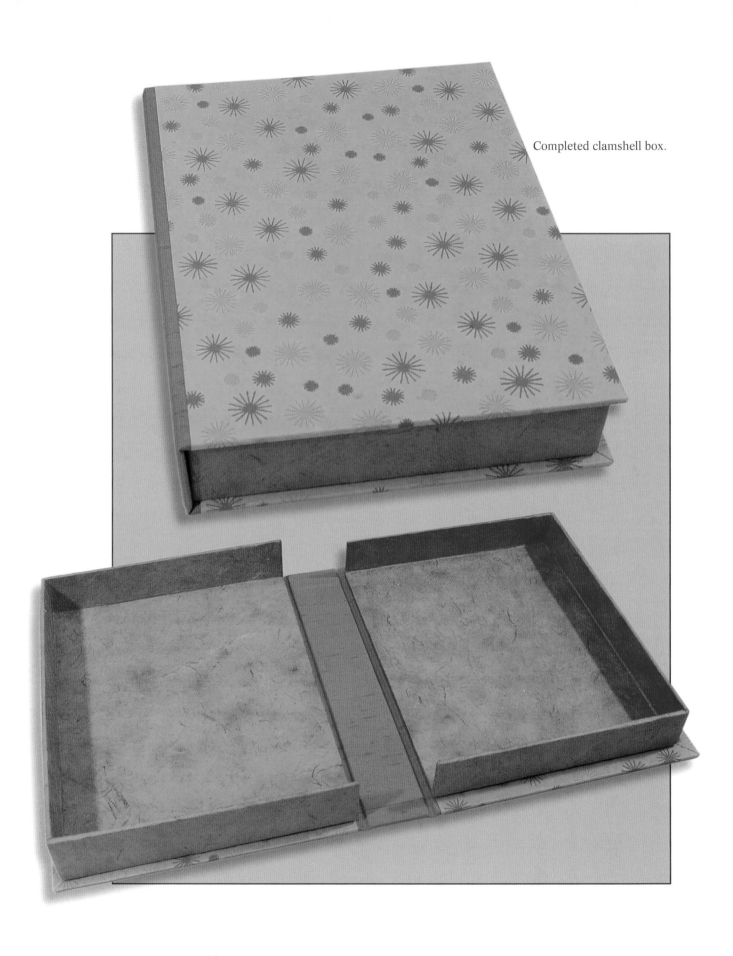

Completed clamshell box.

This chapter offers examples of box variations, added elements, and creative ideas. We hope that through the many images of boxes in this chapter and throughout the book, you will be inspired to explore, modify, or adapt some of the basic techniques learned in this book.

Divided Jewelry Box with Removable Tray, 8" x 10" x 2 1/2".

Chapter 5
Creative Boxes

Divided Box with tray removed.

View of the support ledge on the inside of the Divided Jewelry Box.

55

Desk Top Five Drawer Chest, 4 3/4" x 16 1/2" x 6 1/2". *Made by Annette Hollander*

Box with Flanged Lid and Ribbon Tab, 3 1/2" x 3 1/2" x 1".

Box showing flange on inside of lid.

Hinged Lid Box with
Leather Spine and Fore
Edge, 5 1/2" x 7 1/2" x 2".

Flush Hinged Lid Box
with Knob and Feet, 5
3/4" x 9" x 3".

Stacking House Box with Roof
Tassel, 4 3/4" x 4 3/4" x 8 1/2".
Made by Annette Hollander

Opposite page:
Flanges on the bottom of each
tray are used to hold the boxes
together when stacked.

Clamshell Box with Ribbon Ties, 10" x 12" x 1 1/2".

Hinged Lid Box with Ribbon Tab, 8 1/2" x 10 1/2" x 1 3/4".

Ribbon tab viewed from the inside of the lid.

Paper Clip Box with Curved Scoop, 2 1/2" x 2 1/2" x 1 1/2".

The paper for this simple box was based on a drawing by our daughter, Jessica, at age 5. She had just gone shopping with Grandma (Annette Hollander) and her brother, Daniel.

Box without lid, 6 1/2" x 6 1/2" x 4 1/2".

Slipcase to hold Six Small Books, 4" x 5 1/2" x 6".

Tissue Box, 4 3/4" x 4 3/4" x 5 1/2".

Waste Basket, 5 1/2" base x 7 1/2" opening x 10" high.
Made by Annette Hollander

Hinged Lid CD Box with Angled Lid, closed, 5" x 10" x 6".

CD Box with
Angled Lid,
open.

Treasure Chest with Domed Lid, closed. 5 1/4" x 8 1/4" x 5 1/2".
Made by Annette Hollander

Treasure
Chest,
open.

Shoe Box Style Box,
closed, 6 1/2" x 8 1/2"
x 4 3/4".

Box-in-a-Box, closed, 8 1/2" x 11" x 3".

Box-in-a-Box, open.

Hinged Lid Box of Old New York City, closed, 8" x 10" x 2".

Old New York City Box, open.

Shoe Box Style Box, open.

61

Desktop Caddy,
5 1/2" x 18" x 12".

Old World Shelf Box,
5" x 18" x 18".

Marble Pillar, 6" x 6" x 30".

Divided Playing Card Box,
4 1/4" x 6" x 1 1/4".

Divided Box for Note Pads
and Pencils, 2" x 5" x 3".

Jewelry Box with Removable Trays, 11" x 11" x 1 3/4".
Made by Annette Hollander

Box with several trays removed.

Chess Board with Divided Box, closed, 15" x 15" x 1/4" board, 5" x 13" x 1 1/2" box.

Chess Board with Divided Box, open.

Papyrus Box with Egyptian Painting, closed, 10" x 13" x 2 1/2".

Papyrus Box, open.

Hinged Lid Box with Fish Paper Onlay, 3" x 7" x 1 1/2".

Before proceeding in this section there are a number of important considerations regarding the formulas we use.

1. Although boxes are three-dimensional structures, all the pieces that are cut to construct and cover a box are two-dimensional. Therefore, in the formulas we use, only width and length are indicated. The depth or height of the tray is converted to the width measurement for cutting purposes.

Layout of book board pieces showing two dimensions.

Chapter 6
Box Making Formulas

2. If you are making a hinged lid box to store a particular object such as a book, photo album, or collection of photographs, you will need to consider the space or margin between that item and the four sides of the tray. In most cases it is best to allow 1/4" to 1/2" margin around the object in order to be able to easily remove it from the box. This means that the tray is actually 1/2" to 1" larger than the object in width and length. We have made hinged lid boxes to hold a telephone book, for example, with this additional measurement in mind.

On the other hand, we have also made hinged lid boxes to hold twenty CDs or stationery and measured this box for a tighter fit when the box is filled. In other words, there is flexibility regarding the amount of space you allow.

Hinged Lid Stationery Box, 6 1/2" x 9 1/2" x 2".

3. The clamshell box, or two-tray drop spine box, is the recommended style for a box that offers a tighter fit for an object such as a book. This is possible because the design allows the spine to drop as the box is opened, revealing an open front edge in the two trays, which enables you to easily remove the object. When making a clamshell box, we measure the width, length, and thickness (depth) of the book precisely, and then add a narrower margin, such as 1/16" to 1/8" of space.

Clamshell Box, closed, 6 3/4" x 8 1/2" x 1 1/2".

Clamshell Box with Journal, open. 8 1/2" x 15" x 1 1/2".

4. The starting point for calculating all formulas is called the base measurement. This is determined from an object you either want to place in the box, such as a book, or a predetermined size that you have chosen for your measurements. From the base measurements, specific formulas have been calculated as a guideline for all measurements.

5. The direction of the grain in the formulas is indicated by the number that is underscored in the example measurements listed below each formula. The grain runs parallel to the measurement with the underscored number.

6. The measurements in the paper and book cloth formulas are guidelines. We often will round up or down 1/16" to the nearest 1/8" increment. An exception would be if the paper we are cutting needs to be a precise fit, such as the paper lining the inside of a lid or the bottom of a tray. Book board measurements, however, need to be precise.

Hinged Lid Box Formulas

Hinged Lid Box, 4" x 6" x 1 3/4".

Base Measurement
___ **Width (W) x** ___ **Length (L) x** ___ **Depth (D)**
Example: 5" x <u>7</u>" x 1 3/4"

(*Layout: the authors would prefer that the following formulas numbered 1., 2., 3., etc. be on a single line and not covering 2 lines. However, they do not wish to have the type face reduced further.)

Book Board Formulas
1. Tray Bottom = Base Measurement (W) x Base Measurement (L)
___ (W) x ___ (L)
Example: Tray Bottom = 5" x <u>7</u>"
Quantity: 1

2. Tray Long Sides = Base Measurement (D) x Tray Bottom (L)
___ (W) x ___ (L)
Example: Long Side = 1 3/4" x <u>7</u>"
Quantity: 2

3. Tray Short Sides = Base Measurement (D) x Tray Bottom (W) + 3/16"
___ (W) x ___ (L)
Example: Short Side = 1 3/4" x <u>5 3/16</u>"
Quantity: 2

4. Lid (Cover) = Tray Bottom (W) + 3/8" x Tray Bottom (L) + 1/2"
___ (W) x ___ (L)
Example: Lid = 5 3/8" x <u>7 1/2</u>"
Quantity: 2

5. Spine = Tray Long Side (D) + 1/16" x Lid (L)
___ (W) x ___ (L)
Example: Spine = 1 13/16" x <u>7 1/2</u>"
Quantity: 1

Outside Decorative Paper Formulas
6. Lid/Outside Paper = Lid/Board (W) + 5/8" x Lid/Board (L) + 1 1/2"
___ (W) x ___ (L)
Example: Lid/Outside Paper = 6" x <u>9</u>"
Quantity: 2

7. Spine/Outside Paper = Spine/Board (W) – 1/4" x Spine/Board (L) + 1 1/2"
___ (W) x ___ (L)
Example: Spine/Outside Paper = 1 9/16" x <u>9</u>"
Quantity: 1

8. Long Sides/Outside Paper = Long Sides/Board (W) + 1" x Long Sides/Board (L) + 1 1/4"
___ (W) x ___ (L)
Example: Long Sides/Outside Paper = 2 3/4" x <u>8 1/4</u>"
Quantity: 2

9. Short Sides/Outside Paper = Short Sides/Board (W) + 1" x Bottom/Board (W) – 1/8"
___ (W) x ___ (L)
Example: Short Sides/Outside Paper = 2 3/4" x <u>4 7/8</u>"
Quantity: 2

Inside Decorative Papers Formulas
10. Long Sides/Inside Paper = Long Sides/Board (W) x Long Sides/Board (L) – 1/8"
___ (W) x ___ (L)
Example: Long Side/Inside Paper = 1 3/4" x <u>6 7/8</u>"
Quantity: 2

11. Short Sides/Inside Paper = Short Sides/Board (W) x Bottom/Board (W) + 1/2"
___ (W) x ___ (L)
Example: Short Sides/Inside Paper = 1 3/4" x <u>5 1/2</u>"
Quantity: 2

12. Bottom/Inside Paper = Bottom/Board (W) – 1/8" x Bottom/Board (L) – 1/8"
___ (W) x ___ (L)
Example: Bottom/Inside Paper = 4 7/8" x <u>6 7/8</u>"
Quantity: 1

13. Lid/Inside Paper = Lid/Board (W) – 1/4" x Lid/Board (L) – 3/8"
___ (W) x ___ (L)
Example: Lid/Inside Paper = 5 1/8" x <u>7 1/8</u>"
Quantity: 1

Spine Book Cloth Formulas
14. Outside Spine/Book Cloth = Spine/Board (W) + 1 3/4" x Spine/Board (L) + 1 1/2"
___ (W) x ___ (L)
Example: Outside Spine/Book Cloth = 3 1/2" (rounded down 1/16") x <u>9</u>"
Quantity: 1

15. Inside Spine/Book Cloth = Spine/Board (W) + 1 3/4" x Spine/Board (L) - 1/2"
___ (W) x ___ (L)
Example: Inside Spine/Book Cloth = 3 1/2" (rounded down 1/16") x <u>7</u>"
Quantity: 1

Clamshell Box Formulas

Use a small square and ruler to accurately measure from the spine to the fore edge of the book to accurately determine the measurements for the clamshell box.

In this section we will determine the measurements for making a clamshell box and use as our example a book with the measurements of 5 7/8" (W) x 7 1/4" (L) x 13/16" (D). To determine the base measurement of the clamshell box you will need to add the following to the measurements of an object, or in this case the book.

Add 1/8" to the width (spine to fore edge)*

Add 1/4" to the length (head to tail)

Add 1/4" to the depth (thickness)

To accurately measure the width of a book, it is helpful to use a small square set against the spine, especially if the spine is rounded. Measure the distance from the square to the fore edge of the book. If it is an old book and possibly crooked, you will need to measure the book at its widest and longest points.

Important Note: The formulas listed are for a box with a portrait or vertical orientation only. Boxes that have a landscape or a horizontal orientation will not work with the formulas for cutting the tray sides because instead of two short sides and one long side needed for the trays, you will need two long sides and one short side. You will need to make this adjustment in the formulas for a clamshell box with a landscape orientation.

Base Measurement
____ Width (W) x ____ Length (L) x ____ Depth (D)
Example: 6" x 7 1/2" x 1 1/16"

Book Board Formulas
1. Small Tray Bottom = Base Measurement (W) x Base Measurement (L)
____ (W) x ____ (L)
Example: Small Tray Bottom = 6" x 7 1/2"
Quantity: 1

2. Small Tray Short Sides = Base Measurement (D) x Small Tray Bottom (W)
____ (W) x ____ (L)
Example: Small Tray Short Sides = 1 1/16" x 6"
Quantity: 2

3. Small Tray Long Side = Base Measurement (D) x Small Tray Bottom (L) + 3/16"
____ (W) x ____ (L)
Example: Small Tray Long Side = 1 1/16" x 7 11/16"
Quantity: 1

4. Large Tray Bottom = Small Tray Bottom (W) + 1/4" x Small Tray Bottom (L) + 3/8"
____ (W) x ____ (L)
Example: Large Tray Bottom = 6 1/4" x 7 7/8"
Quantity: 1

5. Large Tray Short Sides = Small Tray Short Side (W) + 3/16" x Large Tray Bottom (W)
____ (W) x ____ (L)
Example: Large Tray Short Sides = 1 1/4" x 6 1/4"
Quantity: 2

6. Large Tray Long Side = Small Tray Long Side (W) + 3/16" x Large Tray Bottom (L) + 3/16"
____ (W) x ____ (L)
Example: Large Tray Long Side = 1 1/4" x 8 1/16"
Quantity: 1

7. Lid (Cover) = Large Tray Bottom (W) + 5/16" x Large Tray Bottom (L) + 1/2"
____ (W) x ____ (L)
Example: Lid = 6 9/16" x 8 3/8"
Quantity: 2

8. Spine = Large Tray Long Side (W) + 1/16" x Lid (L)
____ (W) x ____ (L)
Example: Spine = 1 5/16" x 8 3/8"
Quantity: 1

Decorative Paper Formulas
9. Lid Paper = Lid/Board (W) + 5/8" x Lid/Board (L) + 1 1/2"
____ (W) x ____ (L)
Example: Lid/Outside Paper = 7 1/4" (rounded up 1/16") x 9 7/8"
Quantity: 2

10. Small Tray Short Sides/Paper = (Small Tray Short Sides/Board (W) x 2) + 7/8" x Small Tray Short Sides/Board (L) + 3/4"
____ (W) x ____ (L)
Example: Small Tray Short Sides/Paper = 3" x 6 3/4"
Quantity: 2

11. Small Tray Long Side/Paper = (Small Tray Long Side/Board (W) x 2) + 7/8" x Small Tray Long Side/Board (L) + 1"
____ (W) x ____ (L)
Example: Small Tray Long Side/Paper = 3" x 8 3/4" (rounded up 1/16")
Quantity: 1

12. Small Tray Bottom/Paper = Small Tray Bottom/Board (W) + 3/4" x Small Tray Bottom/Board (L) – 1/8"
____ (W) x ____ (L)
Example: Small Tray Bottom/Paper = 6 3/4" x 7 3/8"
Quantity: 1

13. Large Tray Short Sides/Paper = (Large Tray Short Sides/Board (W) x 2) + 7/8" x Large Tray Short Sides/Board (L) + 3/4"
____ (W) x ____ (L)
Example: Large Tray Short Sides/Paper = 3 3/8" x 7"
Quantity: 2

14. Large Tray Long Side/Paper = (Large Tray Long Side/Board (W) x 2) + 7/8" x Large Tray Long Side/Board (L) + 1"
____ (W) x ____ (L)
Example: Large Tray Long Side/Paper = 3 3/8" x 9" (rounded down 1/16")
Quantity: 1

15. Large Tray Bottom/Paper = Large Tray Bottom/Board (W) + 3/4" x Large Tray Bottom/Board (L) – 1/8"
_____ (W) x _____ (L)
Example: Large Tray Bottom/Paper = 7" x <u>7 3/4"</u>
Quantity: 1

Spine Book Cloth Formulas
16. Outside Spine/Book Cloth = Spine/Board (W) + 1 3/4" x Spine/Board (L) + 1 1/2"
_____ (W) x _____ (L)
Example: Outside Spine/Book Cloth = 3 1/8" (rounded up 1/16") x <u>9 7/8"</u>
Quantity: 1

17. Inside Spine/Book Cloth = Spine/Board (W) + 1 3/4" x Small Tray Bottom/Board (L) + 1/16"
_____ (W) x _____ (L)
Example: Inside Spine/Book Cloth = 3 1/8" (rounded up 1/16") x <u>7 9/16"</u>
Quantity: 1

Formula Worksheets   Use these as worksheets you can photocopy.

<u>Hinged Lid Box Formula Worksheets</u>

Base Measurement = _____ Width (W) x _____ Length (L) x _____ Depth (D)

Book Board
Tray Bottom = Base Measurement (W) x Base Measurement (L)
_____ (W) x _____ (L) Quantity: 1

Tray Long Sides = Base Measurement (D) x Tray Bottom (L)
_____ (W) x _____ (L) Quantity: 2

Tray Short Sides = Base Measurement (D) x Tray Bottom (W) + 3/16"
_____ (W) x _____ (L) Quantity: 2

Lid (Cover) = Tray Bottom (W) + 3/8" x Tray Bottom (L) + 1/2"
_____ (W) x _____ (L) Quantity: 2

Spine = Tray Long Side (D) + 1/16" x Lid (L)
_____ (W) x _____ (L) Quantity: 1

Outside Decorative Papers for Tray
Lid/Outside Paper = Lid/Board (W) + 5/8" x Lid/Board (L) + 1 1/2"
_____ (W) x _____ (L) Quantity: 2

Lid Spine/Outside Paper = Spine/Board (W) – 1/4" x Spine/Board (L) + 1 1/2"
_____ (W) x _____ (L) Quantity: 1

Long Sides/Outside Paper = Long Sides/Board (W) + 1" x Long Sides/Board (L) + 1 1/4"
_____ (W) x _____ (L) Quantity: 2

Short Sides/Outside Paper = Short Sides/Board (W) + 1" x Bottom/Board (W) – 1/8"
_____ (W) x _____ (L) Quantity: 2

Inside Decorative Papers for Tray
Long Sides/Inside Paper = Long Sides/Board (W) x Long Sides/Board (L) – 1/8"
_____ (W) x _____ (L) Quantity: 2

Short Sides/Inside Paper = Short Sides/Board (W) x Bottom/Board (W) + 1/2"
_____ (W) x _____ (L) Quantity: 2

Bottom/Inside Paper = Bottom/Board (W) – 1/8" x Bottom/Board (L) – 1/8"
_____ (W) x _____ (L) Quantity: 1

Lid/Inside Paper = Lid/Board (W) – 1/4" x Lid/Board (L) – 3/8"
_____ (W) x _____ (L) Quantity: 1

Spine Book Cloth for Lid
Outside Spine/Book Cloth = Spine/Board (W) + 1 3/4" x Spine/Board (L) + 1 1/2"
_____ (W) x _____ (L) Quantity: 1

Inside Spine/Book Cloth = Spine/Board (W) + 1 3/4" x Spine/Board (L) - 1/2"
_____ (W) x _____ (L) Quantity: 1

Clamshell Box Formula Worksheets

Base Measurement = _____ Width (W) x _____
Length (L) x _____ Depth (D)

Book Board

**Small Tray Bottom = Base Measurement (W) x
Base Measurement (L)**
_____ (W) x _____ (L) Quantity: 1

**Small Tray Short Sides = Base Measurement (D) x
Small Tray Bottom (W)**
_____ (W) x _____ (L) Quantity: 2

**Small Tray Long Side = Base Measurement (D) x
Small Tray Bottom (L) + 3/16"**
_____ (W) x _____ (L) Quantity: 1

**Large Tray Bottom = Small Tray Bottom (W) + 1/4" x
Small Tray Bottom (L) + 3/8"**
_____ (W) x _____ (L) Quantity: 1

**Large Tray Short Sides = Small Tray Short Side (W) + 3/16" x
Large Tray Bottom (W)**
_____ (W) x _____ (L) Quantity: 2

**Large Tray Long Side = Small Tray Long Side (W) + 3/16" x
Large Tray Bottom (L) + 3/16"**
_____ (W) x _____ (L) Quantity: 1

**Lid (Cover) = Large Tray Bottom (W) + 5/16" x
Large Tray Bottom (L) + 1/2"**
_____ (W) x _____ (L) Quantity: 2

Spine = Large Tray Long Side (W) + 1/16" x Lid (L)
_____ (W) x _____ (L) Quantity: 1

Decorative Papers

Lid Paper = Lid/Board (W) + 5/8" x Lid/Board (L) + 1 1/2"
_____ (W) x _____ (L) Quantity: 2

**Small Tray Short Sides/Paper = (Small Tray Short
Sides/Board (W) x 2) + 7/8" x Small Tray Short
Sides/Board (L) + 3/4"**
_____ (W) x _____ (L) Quantity: 2

**Small Tray Long Side/Paper = (Small Tray Long Side/Board
(W) x 2) + 7/8" x Small Tray Long Side/Board (L) + 1"**
_____ (W) x _____ (L) Quantity: 1

**Small Tray Bottom/Paper = Small Tray Bottom/Board (W) +
3/4" x Small Tray Bottom/Board (L) – 1/8"**
_____ (W) x _____ (L) Quantity: 1

**Large Tray Short Sides/Paper = (Large Tray Short
Sides/Board (W) x 2) + 7/8" x Large Tray Short
Sides/Board (L) + 3/4"**
_____ (W) x _____ (L) Quantity: 2

**Large Tray Long Side/Paper = (Large Tray Long Side/Board
(W) x 2) + 7/8" x Large Tray Long Side/Board (L) + 1"**
_____ (W) x _____ (L) Quantity: 1

**Large Tray/Bottom/Paper = Large Tray/Bottom/Board (W) +
3/4" x Large Tray/Bottom/Board (L) – 1/8"**
_____ (W) x _____ (L) Quantity: 1

Spine Book Cloth for Lid

**Outside Spine/Book Cloth = Spine/Board (W) + 1 3/4" x
Spine/Board (L) + 1 1/2"**
_____ (W) x _____ (L) Quantity: 1

**Inside Spine/Book Cloth = Spine/Board (W) + 1 3/4" x
Small Tray/Bottom/Board (L) + 1/16"**
_____ (W) x _____ (L) Quantity: 1

Glossary of Terms

Acid-Free – Book board and paper that is free from any acid content or other substances likely to have a detrimental effect over time.

Adhesive – A general term used for a number of glues or other bonding materials. See PVA Glue, PVA Thick Glue, Methyl Cellulose, and Glue Gun.

Angled Lid – A style of hinged lid, whereby the front of the lid is cut at a low angle and drapes over the front side of the box. Another style of angled lid is where the two opposite sides of the box are cut at a 45-degree angle to form a gable. The hinged lid sits over the two gabled sides, forming a 45-degree angle.

Binder's Board – See Book Board.

Board Shear – See Board Trimmer.

Board Thickness – Book board can be obtained in various thicknesses in the range of 1/16" to 1/8" thick, but is commonly listed in thousandths of an inch. Typically, book board is available in thicknesses of .060 (approximately 1/16"), .080, or .087 (approximately 3/32"), and .098 (approximately 1/8").

Board Trimmer – Board trimmers are specifically designed for cutting book board. Unfortunately, some of the best models are not being manufactured any longer and the old ones are difficult to find. The one we use in our studio and for workshops is a Jacques Board Shear, which was built in the 1890s.

Book Board – Also referred to as binder's board. It can be obtained in various grades and thicknesses. A standard quality, medium density board is recommended for beginners because it is fairly easy to cut with a utility knife. A higher quality book board, often known as Davey board, is denser and sturdier. See Chip Board, Davey Board, and Mat Board.

Book Cloth – Book cloth is a common covering material used in bookbinding and box making. Traditional book cloth is manufactured with a starch additive that makes it non-porous and durable. Paper-backed cloth, which has become available, more recently, is easier to glue. Because of its durability, book cloth is often used for covering the hinged area along the spine of a box.

Bone Folder – This common and indispensable bookbinding tool is typically used for creasing, pressing, burnishing, and scoring. As a tool for box making, it is used for pressing down paper and book cloth as well as for reaching into corners.

Case – Two lid pieces and a spine joined to form a cover, which is then glued as a unit to the box tray(s) in the same fashion as the cover of a book encasing a text block.

Chip Board – A lower grade book board, generally not acid free.

Clamshell Box – Also referred to as a two-tray drop spine box or portfolio box. This box consists of a pair of three-sided trays, with one constructed slightly larger than the other. Each tray is attached to the lid with the open side facing inward or towards the spine. When the box is opened, the spine drops, allowing the trays to lay flat. When closed, the small tray nests inside the large tray creating a double wall and a solid, highly protective structure.

Clamshell Lid – See Clamshell Box.

Cover – Another name used to describe the lid of a box. Typically it is considered a protective enclosure or casing for a box, consisting of a front and back piece connected by a spine. There are many styles of lids or covers.

Cover Weight – A general term applied to papers slightly heavier than text weight, but not as heavy as card stock.

Covering Material – A number of materials used to cover book board including decorative paper, book cloth, and leather.

Cutting Bar – A heavy, straight edge used for cutting book board with a utility knife.

Cutting Grid – Usually printed on a cutting mat. A large cutting mat with a grid of 1/8" can be used to eliminate the need of measuring and marking a pattern on the back of your materials. This also enables the design of a paper to be seen as you are cutting rather than cutting from a pattern that has been laid out on the backside.

Cutting Knife – The two most important cutting knives used with book board, paper, and book cloth are a heavyweight knife and a lightweight knife. For cutting book board, a heavier knife, such as a utility knife, is essential. A lighter weight cutting knife, such as a #1 or #2 X-acto knife, works well for cutting paper and book cloth.

Cutting Mat – A large, self-healing cutting mat is an ideal surface for board and paper cutting. The synthetic surface allows the mat to "self-heal" after it is cut with a blade. Cutting mats, when kept clean, are a nice surface for working on.

Davey Board – Often used to describe a high quality bookbinding board. Available in varying thicknesses, it is usually single-ply, dense, and warp resistant. The name Davey comes from the company that originally manufactured it.

Decorative Paper – Papers which have some decorative element such as color, texture, or design. Marbled and printed papers are generally used to cover books and boxes, but almost any text weight paper could be used.

Divider – Book board glued to the sides of a tray and bottom to create compartments. Also, a common tool used for measuring.

Divider Guides – Used to measure distance between the inside of a tray side and where the divider will be placed. Used in pairs, both cut to the same size, the divider guides are inserted at each end of the divider, flush to the sides of the tray (and in some cases another divider) and perpendicular to the divider. A divider guide enables you to accurately position the divider. Once the divider is set in place, the guides are removed.

Drop Spine Box – Name given to a clamshell box because the spine drops when the box is opened. See Clamshell Box.

Filler – Paper or thin board cut to the shape of the bare board on the inside of a lid, after the turn-ins have been glued to the inside surface. The filler raises the height of the exposed board to the height of the cover paper so that the lining paper may be applied smoothly to the inside surface, eliminating a visible ridge.

Flanged Lid – A two-piece lid composed of a flange and an overlapping top piece which rests on the top of a box. The flange nests just inside the top edges of the tray, preventing the lid from sliding off the box. The top overlaps the top edges, creating a flush fit.

Floating Lid – A lid which fits just inside the walls of the tray enabling it to "float" up and down, such as on a stack of papers. Often a knob is attached to the center of the floating lid to aid in its removal.

Flush Lid – A lid that sits flush to the outside edges of the box with no overlap.

Folder – See Bone Folder and Teflon folder.

Fore Edge – The front edge of a lid or book, opposite and parallel to the spine edge.

Gap – Space between the spine and spine edge of the lid boards which forms the hinge. Typically, the gap measures twice the thickness of the book board being used.

Glue Gun – A glue gun can be used to quickly glue a lid to a box. Using a glue gun requires accuracy, because the glue dries almost instantly upon contact. A high quality, commercial grade model is recommended.

Grain Direction – The grain direction of book board and paper occurs during the manufacturing process. As the pulp's fibers are being pulled along a conveyor belt, the majority of the fibers align themselves in the direction in which the belt is moving. Book board and paper grain direction is based on the final orientation of these fibers. The parallel alignment of these fibers runs the same direction as the grain.

Grain Long – When the grain is running the length of the material, we call it grain long; when it is running the width, we call it grain short. The same size piece can be either grain long or grain short, depending on the direction of the grain when it is cut.

Grain Short – See Grain Long.

Groove – See Gap, Hinge, or Joint.

Head and Tail – The top and bottom of a box as it stands upright. The names correspond to the head and tail of a book.

Hinge – The space or gap between the spine and the lid boards whereby the lid flexes upon opening and closing. See Gap, Hinge, or Joint.

Hinged Lid – See Hinged Lid Box.

Hinged Lid Box – In this style, the lid is made separately from the tray. The tray is then attached to the bottom of the lid and along the spine. The cover opens and closes along a hinge, much like a cigar box.

Inlay – Created by carefully cutting and peeling off several layers of book board to create a slightly recessed area in the board before covering it and placing an image, text or ephemera in the area that has been cut out.

Inside Paper – Papers, or cloth, used to cover the inside surfaces of a box. See Lining Paper.

Joint – See Hinge or Groove.

Landscape – Box with a horizontal orientation and with the spine attached along the short side of the tray.

Laminate – The process of gluing together two or more pieces of paper or book board to reach a desired thickness.

Lid – The top of a box or, if joined by a spine, the top and bottom covers. See Angled Lid, Clam Shell Lid, Flanged Lid, Floating Lid, Flush Lid, Hinged Lid, and Shoe Box Lid.

Lightweight Paper – Tissue weight and slightly heavier papers, but not as heavy as a text paper.

Lining or Lining Paper – Cover material used on the inside of boxes.

Machine-Made Paper – Paper that is produced on a rapidly moving machine that forms, dries, sizes, presses, and cuts the sheet. This process forms an extremely uniform sheet without deckle edges.

Margin – Term used to designate the distance between two points of reference. For example: (1) the space between the board and the edge of the turn-in, or overlap of paper or book cloth; (2) the space between the inside lining paper and the edge of the lid; or (3) the space between the tray sides and the edges of the lid (See Square).

Mat Board – Commercial board often used in picture framing. It is soft and easy to cut, but thinner than traditional book board.

Measure Twice, Cut Once – Motto used as a reminder to assure accuracy in cutting.

Methyl Cellulose – Powder, mixed with water, and most effective when added to PVA glue to extend the drying time, which allows for repositioning.

Micro Spatula – Long narrow tool with two small spatula shaped ends used to apply glue in a tight area where it is difficult to get to with a brush.

Miter – The corner where a cut has been made at a 45 degree angle, with the goal of reducing the amount of overlapping material. See Tab Miter and V-Shaped Miter.

Onlay – Image, text or ephemera adhered to the outside of a lid or sides of a tray.

Outside Paper – Papers used to cover the outside surfaces of a box.

Overhang – The extending margin, usually between 1/8" and 3/8", of book board between the walls of the tray and the outside edges of the lid. See Square.

Overlap – See Margin and Turn-in.

Paper Cutter – Table paper cutters have a ruler along the top edge and a 1/2" grid marked on the table top for quick measuring and placement of the paper or book cloth. A hinged blade is pulled down across the paper to be cut. A high quality paper cutter is a worthwhile investment if a lot of paper cutting is needed. Our favorite is the Ingento 30" Model with a self-sharpening blade. Although a good paper cutter is great for cutting paper and book cloth, never use a paper cutter to cut book board.

Portrait – Vertical orientation of a box, with the spine attached along the long side of the tray.

Pressing Board – Pressing boards are made of wood, often of finished 3/4" plywood or Plexiglas. They are used to place over the lid of a box, with a heavy weight on top to help assure that the lids dry flat. Usually it is best to allow a piece to dry overnight in this fashion. Large books or other smooth boards combined with heavy weights work well.

PVA Glue – Abbreviation for polyvinyl acetate. This water soluble, white glue is specifically designed to maintain flexibility over time so that it does not become brittle after it dries. It is non-toxic and archival.

PVA Thick Glue – A much thicker and stronger version of regular PVA glue, it works well for specific applications such as box making or where more viscous glue is required to glue the trays together and the tray to the lid.

Ribbon Tab – A short, usually less than ¾", protruding ribbon that can be used to open a box.

Ribbon Tie – Long ribbons, usually 10" to 15" in length, that are attached to lids and that can be used to tie the lids in a closed position.

Shoe Box Style Lid – Separate lid that sits on top of a box. Usually, a shallower tray that is cut to be slightly larger than the usually deeper tray it covers.

Spacer Guide – Spacer Guides are a great aid for making quick and repeated measurements where consistency and accuracy are important. The most common one we use is a 3/16" Spacer Guide, used for measuring the gap that forms the hinge between the spine and lid boards. A number of other guides and jigs may be helpful for various measurements and spacing.

Spine – The center book board piece of a three part hinged lid. On a hinged lid box, the spine is glued to the backside of the tray. On a clamshell box the spine drops down as the box is opened. See Hinged Lid Box and Clamshell Box.

Spine Edge – Edge of the lid board towards the spine and opposite the fore edge.

Spine Gap – Space between the spine and lid boards that forms the hinge.

Square – More commonly known as a measuring tool used for squaring book board and paper. It is also used to denote the extending edge on the lid between the box tray and the edges of the lid.

Straight Edge – A flat metal ruler or cutting bar used as a guide to assure a straight cut with a cutting knife when cutting book board, papers, and book cloth.

Tab – Small or narrow flap formed by cutting paper or book cloth. Tabs are turned in to cover a corner or open edge on a box. Also, see Ribbon Tab.

Tab Miter – Cutting book cloth or paper to leave a small flap that gets turned in. One type of tab, formed with a single cut, wraps around a corner and covers two sides of a tray. Another type is a narrow tab of approximately 1/2" formed from two parallel cuts. Sometimes referred to as Tongue tab, this type is used to cover the inside corner of a tray.

Tail – See Head and Tail.

Tapping – Using the bone folder to tap the corners after they have been mitered and covered. This helps to smooth and eliminate any burrs and is best done soon after gluing, when the cover material is still slightly malleable.

Teflon Folder – Used as an alternative to the standard bone folder. Teflon allows you to use more pressure on delicate papers or book cloth without burnishing.

Text Weight – Text papers have the approximate weight of text pages in a book, or the weight of copy paper. Typical text weight papers we like to use in box making are marbled papers, Florentine prints, Indian silk-screened papers, and many of the decorative papers from Japan.

Thick Glue Applicator – Tool used to apply PVA Thick glue to the edges of book board when constructing a box. The Thick glue applicator tool is one you can easily make using a piece of book board approximately ½" wide by 3" in length. The grain of the board should run along the 3" length for increased strength.

Thick Glue Scraper – Tool used to scrape off excess Thick glue that oozes out along the inside walls of a box as it is being constructed. A makeshift tool made from book board cut approximately ½" x 3" with the grain running long. At one end, make a 45-degree angled cut, leaving a small straight edge of 1/8" at the tip.

Tissue Weight – Papers that are thinner than Text Weight and are normally not recommended for box making.

Tray – In box making, a three- or four-sided structure for holding objects. The tray is constructed separate from a lid.

Tray Bottom – The bottom piece of a tray to which sides (walls) are glued along the edges. The underside of the tray bottom is often glued to a bottom lid. The tray bottom is also referred to as the base.

Tray Sides – Attached to the tray bottom, along the edge of the board, in the form of a butt joint. Sides of a tray are also referred to as walls.

Tucked-In Corner – The slightly inward tuck of a cover material along the mitered edge of the board after the first turn-in. The tuck-in, often accomplished with a bone folder or end of a finger, eliminates a slight burr from forming at the edge of the corner following the second turn-in.

Turn-In – The extra ½" to ¾" length of paper or book cloth that overlaps an open edge of book board. It is folded around the board edge and glued down onto the inside surface.

Two Tray Box – Name sometimes given to describe a clamshell box because it is composed of two trays.

V-Shape Miter – Cutting two edges of paper together at a fold to form a V shape, such as when mitering the outside bottom of a tray.

Wall – Term used to identify the sides of a tray.

Waste Sheet – Blank newsprint, copy paper, or pages from old telephone books used as a disposable sheet under decorative paper or book cloth when applying glue.

Weights – Used to ensure that book board dries flat, especially after paper or book cloth has been glued to a lid. We have used covered bricks, heavy books, shrink-wrapped stacks of legal pads, soft weights, and a number of other flat, heavy objects.

Box Making Resources

Books

We have found the following books to offer sound box making instruction at various levels from the beginner to the more advanced. Overall, they are useful resources.

Brown, Margaret R. and Don Etherington. *Boxes for the Protection of Rare Books: Their Design and Construction.* Washington: Library of Congress, 1982. (Out of Print)

Ferrari, Valeria & Ersilia Fiorucci. *Paper Crafting Beautiful Boxes, Book Covers and Frames.* New York: Sterling Publishing, 1999. (Out of Print)

Hollander, Annette. *Bookcraft.* New York: Van Nostrand Reinhold, 1974. Reprinted as *Easy to Make Decorative Boxes and Desk Accessories.* New York: Dover Publications, 1986. (Out of Print)

Rinehart, Benjamin. *Creating Books and Boxes.* Gloucester, Massachusetts: Quayside Publishing, 2007.

Watson, Aldren. *Hand Bookbinding.* New York: Dover Publishing, 1986.

Webberley, Marilyn and JoAn Forsyth. *Books, Boxes, and Wraps.* Kirkland, Washington: Bifocal Press, 1995.

Young, Laura S. *Bookbinding and Conservation by Hand: A Working Guide.* New York: R.B. Bowker, 1981.

Zeier, Franz. *Books, Boxes, and Portfolios: Binding, Construction, and Design Step by Step.* New York: Design Press, 1990.

Schools and Organizations

Box making workshops are occasionally offered at a number of Book Arts Centers and schools listed below. A basic bookbinding workshop, more widely available, can offer a number of tips, since many of the materials, tools, and techniques are similar. The schools and organizations listed below are a good starting point and can provide information on other resources available.

Workshop at Hollander's.

American Academy of Bookbinding
P.O. Box 1590, 300 S. Townsend Avenue, Telluride, CO 81435
Phone: 970-728-3886
Website: www.ahhaa.org

Canadian Bookbinders & Book Artists Guild (CBBAG)
60 Atlantic Avenue, Suite 112, Toronto, Ontario, Canada M6K 1X9
Phone: 416-581-1071
Website: www.cbbag.ca

The Center for Book Arts
28 West 27th Street, 3rd Floor New York, NY 10001
Phone: 212-481-0295
Website: www.centerforbookarts.org

Columbia College Center for Book and Paper Arts
1104 S. Wabash, 2nd Floor, Chicago, IL 60605
Phone: 312-344-6630
Website: www.colum.edu/Book_and_Paper/

Garage Street Annex
One Cottage Street #5, Room 503, Easthampton, MA 01027
Phone: 413 527-8044
Website: www.garageannexschool.com

Guild of Bookworkers
521 Fifth Avenue, New York, NY 10175-0083
Website: http://palimpsest.stanford.edu/byorg/gbw/index.shtml

Hollander's School of Book & Paper Arts
410 North Fourth Avenue, Ann Arbor, MI 48104
Phone: 734-741-7531
Website: www.hollanders.com

Minnesota Center for Book Arts (MCBA)
1011 Washington Avenue, Minneapolis, MN 55415
Phone: 612-338-3634
Website: www.mnbookarts.org

San Francisco Center for the Book
300 DeHaro Street, San Francisco, CA 94103
Phone: 415-565-0545
Website: www.sfcb.org

Suppliers

There are many art and craft supply stores that carry some of the basic tools needed for box making such as scissors, brushes, and cutting knives. However, some supplies such as book board and book cloth may be more difficult to find. We have listed some of the more reliable suppliers we know of. Searching the Internet using bookbinding tools or bookbinding supplies as key words may be helpful.

Bookmakers International, LTD
8601 Rhode Island Avenue, College Park, MD 20740
Phone: 301-345-7979
Website: www.bookmakerscatalog.com
Source for bookbinding tools and supplies.

Colophon Book Arts Supply
3611 Ryan Street SE, Lacy, WA 98503
Phone: 360-459-2940
Website: www.colophonbookarts.com
Source for bookbinding tools and supplies.

Hollander's
410 North Fourth Ave, Ann Arbor, MI 48104
Phone: 734-741-7531
Website: www.hollanders.com
Source for bookbinding tools and supplies, decorative papers, board cutting services, box making and bookbinding kits.

The Japanese Paper Place
77 Brock Avenue, Toronto, Ontario, Canada M6K 2L3
Phone: 416-538-9669
Website: www.japanesepaperplace.com
Source for Japanese decorative papers.

John Neal, Bookseller
1833 Spring Garden Street, Greensboro, NC 27403
Phone: 336-272-6139
Website: www.johnnealbooks.com
Source for bookbinding tools and supplies.

Lineco Inc.
P.O. Box 2604, Holyoke, MA 01041
Phone: 800-322-7775
Website: www.lineco.com
Source for bookbinding tools and supplies.

Kate's Paperie
460 West 34th Street, 3rd Floor, New York, NY 10001
Phone: 800-809-9880
Website: www.katespaperie.com
Source for decorative papers.

Paper Source
410 N. Milwaukee, Chicago, IL 60610
Phone: 888-paper11
Website: www.paper-source.com
Source for decorative papers.

Talas
20 West 20th Street, 5th Floor, New York, NY 10011
Phone: 212-219-0770
Website: www.talasonline.com
Source for bookbinding tools and supplies.

Appendix

Approximate Conversions

Fractional to Decimal
1/32"	=	.030
1/16"	=	.060
3/32"	=	.090
1/8"	=	.125
3/16"	=	.180
1/4"	=	.250
5/16"	=	.300
3/8"	=	.375
7/16"	=	.430
1/2"	=	.500
9/16"	=	.560
5/8"	=	.625
11/16"	=	.680
3/4"	=	.075
15/16"	=	.930
1"	=	1.00

Fractional to Metric (mm)
1/32"	=	.75
1/16"	=	1.5
3/32"	=	2.5
1/8"	=	3.0
3/16"	=	4.5
1/4"	=	6.0
5/16"	=	7.5
3/8"	=	9.5
7/16"	=	11.0
1/2"	=	12.5
9/16"	=	14.0
5/8"	=	16.0
11/16"	=	17.5
3/4"	=	19.0
13/16"	=	20.5
7/8"	=	22.0
15/16"	=	23.5
1"	=	25.0

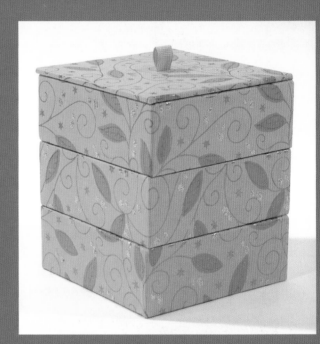